PALESTINE: A Question of History

Unearthing the Truth about the Israeli-Palestinian Conflict
Yosef Rabin

INTRODUCTION

Israel has been condemned...on the streets, within the halls of the United Nations, and before the ICJ (The International Court of Justice) because of a legal view rooted deeply in a specific historical narrative. Namely, in 1948, the Jews came to a foreign land, colonized it, ethnically cleansed it, and then occupied it for the last 75 years.

But does this bold claim meet the test of history? Does the Palestinian claim of ancient nationhood meet the same rigorous standards as the claim of the Jews? What evidence supports or undermines such a grand assertion?

This question has been asked like never before following the events of October, 7th, 2023. On this day, Hamas coordinated a shocking and stunning blitzkrieg-style attack against Israel. Around 6:30 a.m., 3,000 rockets were launched into Southern Israel without warning. Hamas, a terrorist group elected by Gazans in 2007, decided to attack Israel ruthlessly, foregoing any resemblance of peace and negotiation. This was not an impromptu decision. After years of careful planning, Hamas soldiers stormed southern Israel by hang gliders, motorbikes, and speedboats. All of this taking place on Simchat Torah, a most festive Jewish holiday that takes place during the festival of Sukkot.

Hamas Turns Nova from a Festival of Joy to one of Rape and Slaughter. (Hamas GoPro Cam)

This day would be known as "Black Saturday" to the Israeli people, not because of the rocket barrage—they were used to being bombarded—but due to the ruthless and heinous attacks carried out by Hamas soldiers on military and civilians alike. Over a thousand people were murdered, including nearly 700 Israeli civilians and over 30 children. Hostages were taken, even women and children. Widespread reports of horrific acts of rape and sexual assault were committed. Babies were burned alive and decapitated. Meanwhile, Hamas proudly live-streamed this modern-day Nazi horror show for all the world to see.

Hamas Setting Israeli Cars with Their Passengers on Fire in a Horrific Display of Barbarism (Hamas GoPro Cam)

As the Hamas footage went viral, thousands of Gazan civilians, including men, women, and children, poured over the border into Israeli towns to loot, burn, rape, kill, and torture. Yes, even children were seen on camera lugging jerrycans of gasoline to burn down Jewish homes. Meanwhile, back in Gaza, masses gathered in the streets to revel as stripped Jewish female captives were paraded as victory trophies. The 7th of October was not just a Hamas massacre, but a popular Palestinian pogrom against the Jews.

**Gazans Celebrate as Israeli Hostages are Brought into the Strip.
(Photo Taken by Local Gazans)**

" Innocent and Uninvolved" Gazan Mobs Mercilessly Beat Kidnapped Israelis after Being Brought into the Strip. (Photo Taken by Local Gazans)

It was revealed that Hamas had been planning the attack for around two years. According to the New York Times, intricate details about Israeli military bases, targets and operational plans had been found, and "Hamas followed the blueprint with shocking precision." To further bring home this point, it was reported that Hamas had breached the border fence of Israel in over 30 individual locations!

Not Just Hamas, but Regular Gazan Men, Young and Old, Pour over the Fence to Murder, Rape and Loot. (Hamas GoPro Cam)

Shocked and horrified, Israel declared war, and on October 9th, they had no choice but to cut off water, electricity, food, and fuel from the Gaza Strip, but even in a state of war, Israel put more care into the Palestinians than their so-called leaders.

Israel did not match fire with fire. They asked residents to evacuate entire neighborhoods to avoid the conflict. Roads were shut down to prevent Gaza citizens from wandering into the warfare. Targets were carefully considered and bases were not taken over until it was determined whether they were in control of Hamas or Israeli soldiers.

Hostages were taken, but only of Hamas soldiers, and they were not executed, but interrogated. The Israeli office of the Israeli Attorney General even inspected the prisons to ensure that Hamas and Gazan murderers and rapists were being held in accordance with the law. A far cry from how Hamas treated Israeli victims. Occasionally, there were halts in the fighting to allow exchanges of hostages, and even then, Israel was more generous. Over a seven-day pause, 110 Israeli hostages were exchanged for 240 Palestinian terrorists and security prisoners.

What was the justification that Hamas gave for their unprecedented barbaric assault? Their answer: the Israeli occupation of Palestinian territory.

Hamas and Gazans Invade Jewish Villages on October 7th.
(Hamas GoPro Cam)

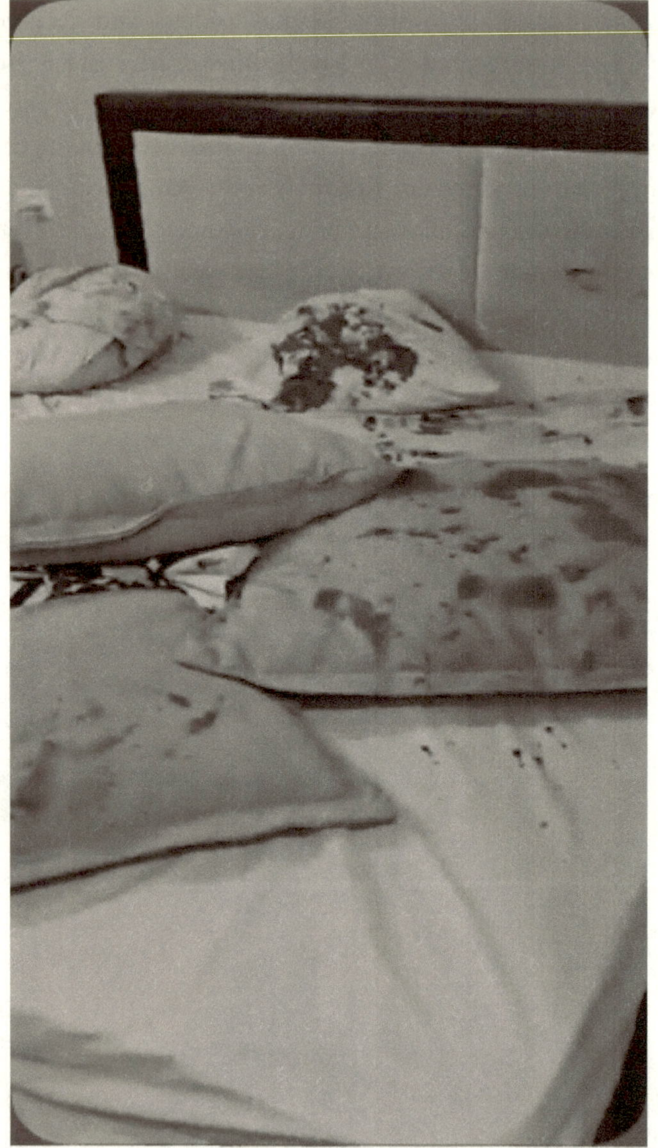

Israelis Slaughtered in Their Own Beds. (Hamas GoPro Cam)
While any sane person would decry the horrific actions committed
on October 7th, there is still widespread sympathy for the concept
of "resisting occupation." The conversation always goes something like

this "The conflict did not begin on October 7th, it started with the occupation of Palestine in 1948."

Only 44 nations, including the United States, the UK, France, Italy, and others denounced Hamas and spoke against their atrocities. Other countries such as Saudi Arabia, Syria, Iran, Iraq, Turkey, Russia, China, and others either blamed Israel or refused to condemn Hamas. Even UN Women declined for months to condemn the sexual assaults on Israeli women by Hamas and their Gazan supporters! This was in line with prominent feminist and gender studies academic, Judith Butler, who defended the mass rape of Israeli women as simply "armed resistance."

On April 18th, 2024, just six months after October 7th, the United Nations Security Council gathered to vote on the Palestinian bid to be recognized as a full member state at the United Nations. The United States vetoed with 12 votes in favor and 2 abstentions. The US vetoed only because it believed that a Palestinian State could only be declared via negotiations with Israel.

However, even this tactical support of Israel is in trouble.

As of March 2024, only 58% of Americans have a "favorable view of Israel," which is "the lowest favorable rating of Israel in over two decades." Palestine sits at 18%, which marks nearly a fifth of Americans in support of them, even after the October 7th attacks!

It gets even worse when taking the next generation into account. 18–34-year-olds only view Israel favorably at 38% and shockingly, favor Palestine at 32%! What will it mean for the future of Israel if one of its closest allies begins to see them on the same level as their greatest threat?

Israel is not only in trouble on the world political stage but also on the legal one as well.

As of January 2024, the International Court of Justice, in a 15-2 ruling, stated that "at least some of Israel's actions in the Gaza Strip during the ongoing war against Hamas could fall within the terms of the Genocide Convention...and [therefore Israel must] take a series of preventative measures." Even though Israel is acting in clear self-defense and merely responding to Hamas, they are being hamstrung. Prime Minister Benjamin Netanyahu stated, "the vile attempt to deny Israel this fundamental right is blatant discrimination against the Jewish state."

Countries and legal bodies alike almost see the 7th of October as some sort of semi-legitimate tantrum thrown by Hamas for Israel's occupation of their land.

In its advisory opinion in 2023, the International Court of Justice opined:

"Legal consequences arising from the ongoing violation by Israel of the right of the Palestinian people to self-determination, from its prolonged occupation, settlement and annexation of the Palestinian territory since, including measures aimed at altering the demographic composition, character and status of the Holy City of Jerusalem, and from its adoption of related discriminatory legislation and measures."

– ICJ advisory, 2023

Additionally, the United Nations Independent International Commission of Inquiry in 2022, reported that "by continuing to occupy the territory by force, Israel incurs international responsibilities and remains accountable for violations of the rights of the Palestinians individually and as a people." The report goes into the poor conditions of the Palestinian people and their plight, ignoring how Hamas and other terrorist organizations that have occupied their own areas, thus denying their own people proper care, food, water, and supplies. They further use their war against Israel to ensure their own peoples' continued suffering.

Based on the report, it said that there may be "reasonable grounds to conclude that Israeli occupation of Palestinian territory is now unlawful under international law due to its permanence and the Israeli Government's de-facto annexation policies."

However, the international political and legal community refuses to understand that the accepted legal view of Israel as an occupier is based on a problematic historical narrative. Are the Palestinians truly an ancient people with deep roots in the holy land, or a 20th-century creation with the sole goal of stopping the creation of a Jewish State?

Chapter 1: Lineage Deep Roots

Everyone has a little common knowledge when it comes to the origins of the Jews. The Torah (Jewish Bible) explains how the Jewish people are descendants of the Hebrews (also referenced in the Christian and Islamic scriptures). Israelites from the nomadic era were generally referred to as Hebrews because of their ties to the Father of Nations, Abraham. The word, Hebrew or "Ivri," has ties to meanings such as "beyond or across" and Greek translations to "one who came across, or a migrant." The term was often used by those that were not Israelites, such as the Egyptians. The Hebrews did not refer to themselves by this name at first. The word "Israel" was first mentioned circa 1208 BCE in the Merneptah Stele via hieroglyphs, an inscription by a pharaoh who presided over Egypt from 1213 to 1203 BCE.

As a nomadic people, they were constantly on the move, searching for a home in the tradition of their father, Abraham, a man called by God to leave his father's house and settle in a land that would become Israel. The 12 tribes of Abraham's great-grandchildren, the children of Jacob, would eventually become enslaved for 210 years after a severe famine forced them to relocate to Egypt. After escaping bondage under the leadership of Moses, they wandered the wilderness for 40 years, going through many tribulations. After Moses's passing, Joshua led the 12 tribes of Israel over the Jordan River back into the land of their forefathers.

THE TWELVE TRIBES
OF ISRAEL
Around 1200-1050 B.C.
(according to the Book of Joshua)
(km)
0
100
(mi)
0
60
Mediterranean
Sea
Sidon
ARAMEANS
Ijon
Tyre
Dan
ASHER
Kedesh
NAPHTALI
Hazor
Chinnereth
Ashteroth
Achshaph
Hamath
BASAN
Helkath
ZEBULUN
Mount Tabor
Jokneam
Edrei
Dor
ISSACHAR
Japhia
Camon
Megiddo
Jezreel
Taanach
Bethshean
Ramoth-Gilead
MANASSEH
Tirzah
Shamir
Zaphon
River Jordan
Shechem
Mahanaim
Pirathon
Gathrimmon
Aphek
Shiloh
GAD
AMMON
Joppa
EPHRAIM
Jazer
Rabbath Ammon
DAN
Bethel
Bethoron
Ai
Gilgal
Eltekeh
Gezer
Heshbon
Mephaath
Gibeon
Gibbethon
Jericho
BENJAMIN
Bezer
Ashdod
Ekron
Jerusalem
Mount Nebo
Bethlehem
Ashkelon
Gath
Jarmuth
REUBEN
PHILISTIA
Lachish
JUDAH
Jahaza
Gaza
Hebron
Debir
Dead Sea
Eshtemoa
Gerar
Arad
Beersheba
MOAB
SIMEON
Kirhareseth
AMALEK
Zoar
Wilderness of
Zin
EDOM
Tamar
Zalmona
Bozrah
Kadesh
Punon

Under the Leadership of Joshua, the Land is Conquered and Divided along the 12 Tribes of Israel. (1)

For nearly 400 years, the tribes lived under a system of Judges before unifying into a single Kingdom under Kings Saul, David, and Solomon. It was during this 120-year unification in 1000 BCE that Jerusalem was declared the capital, and the Holy Temple was built there to symbolize the covenant between Israel and God.

THE UNITED KINGDOM OF ISRAEL
Around the time of
SAUL AND DAVID
EDOM Vassals and defeated peoples
(km)
(mi)
0
100
0
60
Sidon
ARAMEANS
Iion
Dan
Tyre
Cedes
Mediterranean
Sea
Hazor
Kinneret
Astarot
Acsaf
Cammat
Helcat
Mount Tabor
Edrei
Jocneam
Kamon
Dor
Jafia
Megiddo
Jezreel
Ramoth Galaad
Taanach
Beit She'an
KINGDOM OF
ISRAEL
Tirza
Samir
Zafon
Siquem
Mahanaim
Piraton
River Jordan
Gat-Rimon
Afec
Silo
AMON
Jaffa
Jazer
Betel
Gilgal
Rabbath Amon
Elteke
Bet-Horon
Ai
Gezer
Gabaon
Jericho
Gibeton
Hesbon
Mefaat
Ashdod
Ekron
Beser
Jerusalem
Mount Nebo
Ashkelon
Gat
Bethlehem
Jarmut
PHILISTIA
Laquis
Gaza
Jahaza
Hebron
Debir
Estemoa
Gerar
Beersheba
Arad
Dead Sea
MOAB
Kir-Hareset
AMALEC
Zoar
Wilderness of
Zin
EDOM
Tamar
Zalmona
Bosra
Kadesh
Punon

The United Kingdom of Israel under Kings Saul, David and Solomon (2)

After King Solomon passed away, the ten northern tribes did not want to be ruled under his son, Rehoboam and this was when two Kingdoms were formed instead of one monarchy (such as under King Saul or King David). Divided and small, these two Kingdoms were ripe for targeting by other nations.

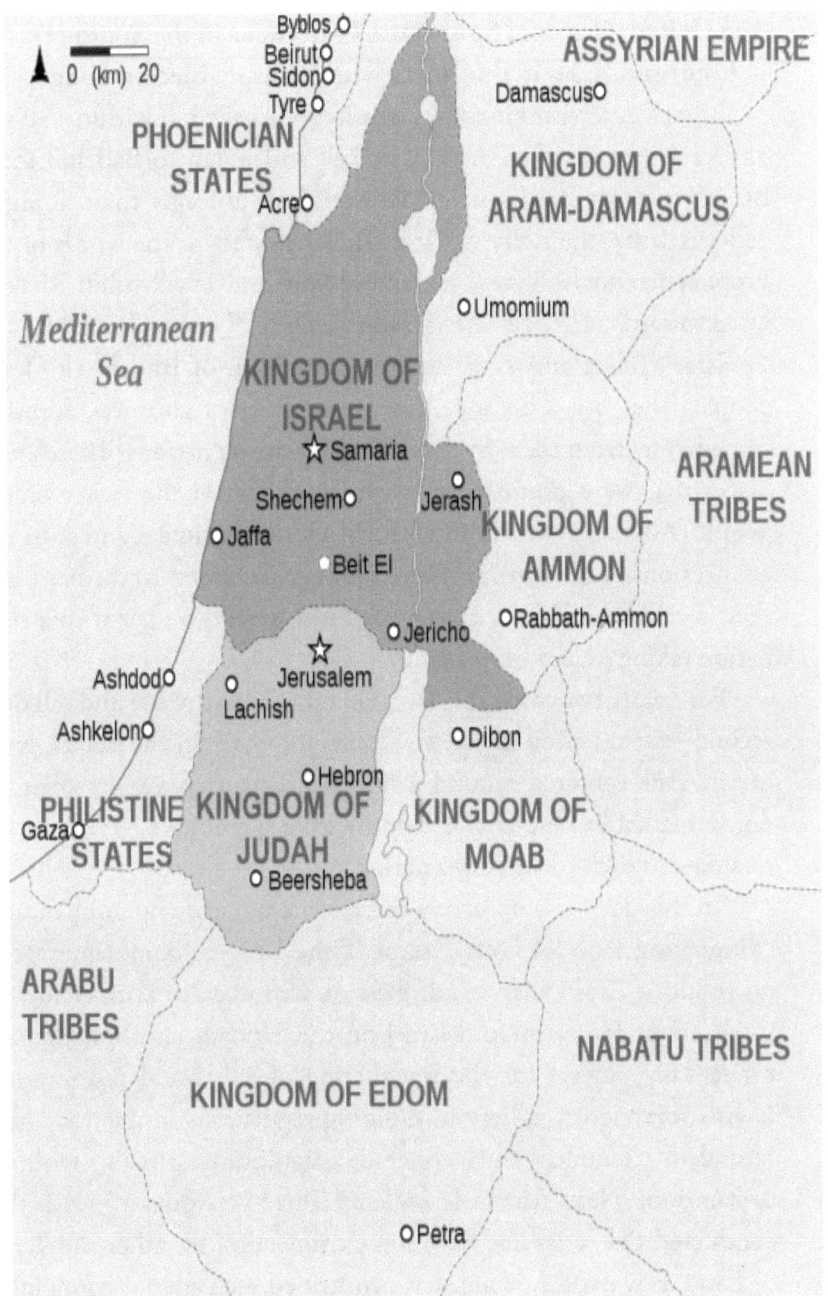
0 (km) 20
Byblos
Beirut
Sidon
Tyre
PHOENICIAN
STATES
Acre
ASSYRIAN EMPIRE
Damascus
KINGDOM OF
ARAM-DAMASCUS
Mediterranean
Sea
Umomium
KINGDOM OF
ISRAEL
Samaria
Shechem
Jerash
ARAMEAN
TRIBES
KINGDOM OF
AMMON
Jaffa
Beit El
Rabbath-Ammon
Jericho
Ashdod
Jerusalem
Lachish
Ashkelon
Dibon
Hebron
PHILISTINE
STATES
Gaza
KINGDOM OF
JUDAH
Beersheba
KINGDOM OF
MOAB
ARABU
TRIBES
NABATU TRIBES
KINGDOM OF EDOM
Petra

The United Kingdom Splits into Two: Judea in the South (Davidic Line) and Israel in the North with Multiple Elected Kings. (3)

The twin Jewish kingdoms would eventually fall within 130 years of each other, Israel to Assyria in 722 and Judah to Babylon in 586 BCE. However, the Jews in exile would never forget their homeland or Jerusalem—their city of God. They held fast to the words of their Prophet Jeremiah: "I will remember you, and I will fulfill My good word toward you, to restore you to this place." (Jeremiah 29:10)

Israel, Judea and Zion are not just pieces of land to the Jewish people. They are a heritage, lineage and legacy that was eventually ripped away from them by other larger, warring nations. These are the places that were promised to them by God and the father of their people (Abraham) which brings forth a lot of sentiment and passionate connections. It is the place where they can be closest to the heritage of their forefathers. Taking Zion away from Israel is on par with a ruling nation taking Mecca from Islam.

For nearly two millennia (we will talk about the rise and fall of the second Jewish period of Jewish sovereignty later in the book), Jewish life in exile centered around a homeland many never set their eyes on. Remarkably, despite this lengthy exile spanning 1,879 years, Jews maintained their identity as a nation.

To this day, Jews observe a three-week mourning period annually, culminating in a 24-hour fast of Tisha b'Av, to commemorate the downfall of Zion; they break glass at weddings to temper joy, sing songs about Jerusalem and Israel on the Sabbath and holidays, offer thrice-daily prayers for the ingathering of exiles and restoration of Jewish sovereignty, adhere to building regulations in memory of the Jerusalem Temple, and conclude significant rituals with the declaration, "Next Year in Jerusalem." There is seldom a Jewish ritual conducted that does not have some connection to either the Temple or Land. Few nations, if any, have enshrined such a fervent longing for their ancient homeland.

Israel is a nation that has not lost its connection to its homeland, even after many exiles and displacements, and the numbers speak for themselves. According to Pew Research, a whopping 92% of Jewish People from the ultra-Orthodox to ultra-secular, view the survival of a strong Israel as necessary for the continuity of the Jewish People.

When was the last time an issue was in almost universal agreement across ages, education, and political affiliation? It is clear that having a Jewish homeland is essential to their very identity, and all of this can be traced through the extensive and rich history that defines its people.

Chapter 2 – Jewish Sovereignty 1273 BCE to 587

The Jewish people are resilient, having faced many obstacles in their journey to the holy land. Though Abraham is considered the founder of the Jewish people, it is Moses who would be revered as her most notable prophet. Moses was born when the Israelites were a minority, enslaved, and yearning for change at the hands of the Egyptians. The descendants of Abraham were starting to grow in population and the Pharoah began to wonder if these people would try to free themselves, either through revolt or allying themselves with Egypt's enemies. It is said that God chose Moses (and his brother Aaron) to address Pharoah and seek out the freedom of the Israelites. After plagues from God and much pleading, Pharoah eventually (and reluctantly) let the Israelites go. It would take another 40 years of wandering through the desert for the Israelites to find the "Promised Land," but they were a nomadic people, known to be hard-working and determined.

To keep the Promised Land secure and to prevent it from invasion and occupation, the Israelites, led by Judges, were in a constant state of conflict on how to keep the Promised Land secure and to prevent it from invasion and occupation. This remained the case until Saul. This was the first major transition from Israelites as nomads to becoming a Kingdom and a nation. This was a pivotal event in Jewish history because, unlike many other nations that had established lands in which they were born, the Israelites were nomads in search of a home. They had been promised one by God, but there had been suffering, enslavement, and many pitfalls on that journey. The Israelites wanted a land of their own and had no desire to conquer others and expand their borders. The land of Israel, even to this day, is very small, about the size of Connecticut in the United States.

After Saul's tumultuous reign, his son-in-law, David, said to have heart after God's took over the throne, said to have a heart after God's. Known for his defeat over Goliath and being the author of Psalms, King David is to this day, the most beloved Jewish King. His Book of Psalms is still recited by Jews worldwide, especially in times of distress.

Legends and stories attributed to him spread even throughout Christianity and Islam. Solomon, his son and the next King, was almost just as well-known as his father. Solomon built the First Temple in Jerusalem, was acclaimed for his great wisdom, and established his United Israel as a military powerhouse with alliances, trade, and tremendous construction projects. Unfortunately, it is his legacy that ends in tragedy.

After his death, his son Rehoboam took over and decided against the advice of his council to raise taxes significantly, threatening: "My little finger is thicker than my father's loins." (Kings 1:12) Angry mobs across the kingdom stoned tax collectors, even killing some. Rehoboam gathered an army of 180,000 men to restore order. However, right before the marching orders were given, Shemiya, a respected prophet, warned the king that civil war would only anger God. Rehoboam relented, and the 10 tribes of the north established their own independent Jewish kingdom, anointing Jeroboam as their King. The Kingdoms of Judah in the South and Israel in the North would never again reunite, leaving both open to outside threats, which eventually led to their downfall.

For example, during Rehoboam's fifth year as King, Shishak, king of Egypt, invaded and occupied a number of cities between Gezer and Gibeon, cutting off a valuable trade route from South Arabia and leaving the two Jewish Kingdoms in financial straits. To appease Shishak, Rehoboam gave him all of the treasures in the temple, which outraged the people. It is doubtful that Egypt would have organized such an attack in the days of Solomon or David when Israel sat under one united Kingdom.

In 722 BCE, The Northern Kingdom of Israel would be the first to fall, after an invasion by the Assyrian Empire led by King Saragon II. The majority of the Jewish tribes—Asher, Dan, Ephraim, Gad, Issachar, Manasseh, Naphtali, Reuben, Simeon, and Zebulun—were exiled and their land was desolated. However, the Fate of Judah, Benjamin and some Levis (the priestly class) in the South was not far behind, coming just 136 years later.

Nebuchadnezzar, King of Neo-Babylon took over the Israelite city of Askelon and demanded a tax from the Kingdom of Judea in exchange for a halt to the invasion. King Jehoiakim, the King of Judah at the time, was already paying a tax to the Pharoah of Egypt, so he tried to get the Pharoah to assist him in defeating Nebuchadnezzar.

It went poorly.

King Jehoiakim was killed and his 18-year-old son was appointed King. Months later, Nebuchadnezzar arrived in Jerusalem, placing the young boy's uncle in charge instead, but not before ransacking the city. The uncle (Zedekiah), now King, tried his hand at rebellion, but again, it too ended in failure.

This all culminated in the siege of Jerusalem circa 589-587 BCE, in which the Neo-Babylonians under King Nebuchadnezzar II invaded Jerusalem, and after a long battle, razed the city and the Holy Temple at its center on the 9th of the Hebrew month of Av. With the Kingdom of Judah decimated, many of the survivors were exiled to Babylon, and for the first time in 800 years - the entire land of Israel, from north to south, was bereft of its children.

However, even in exile, far away from home, the children of Israel never ceased to believe that they would return.

Chapter 3 – Jewish Sovereignty 352 BCE – 69 CE

It was not until the Neo-Babylonians were conquered by the Persian Empire that the Jews received permission by royal decree to return home. Around 539 BCE, Cyrus the Great, King of Persia, decided that the Jews should be allowed to return to Judah under the Edict of Cyrus. This allowed the Jews to not only reclaim their land but to also establish Jewish Autonomy in Jerusalem and its outlying areas under the Persian empire. In the initial ascent to Jerusalem, over 50,000 Jews returned under the leadership of two revered Rabbis named Ezra and Nechemya.

Excitement gripped the Jewish exiles throughout the Persian empire. Even those who did not immediately return to the land donated gold and silver to aid in the rebuilding of Jerusalem and the Holy Temple. As the Jews gathered once again to celebrate this revival, "The people could not distinguish the shouts of joy from the people's weeping." (Ezra 13:3).

While the young sang and danced in ecstasy, the older generation, who still remembered the exile just 70 years prior wailed with tears. The new modest Temple was but a shadow of the grand Temple of Solomon they remembered as young children.

But they knew that God would once again dwell among them. As the Jews began settling back home, they switched their Babylonian names for Jewish ones, intermarriage with non-Jewish women ceased, and their Jewish existence once again began to take on a national form.

With the second temple erected, festivals and traditions were once again renewed in and around Jerusalem like in the days of old. Jews from all over the region would travel back to the holy city to participate in the Biblical pilgrimages of Passover, Shavuot, and Sukkot.

Over the next 400 years, the Second Temple would not only go through expansions and renovations but would far exceed the grandeur of Solomon's Temple. The walls of Jerusalem were rebuilt, and the construction of its former glory began in a long, arduous process.

Around 332 B.C.E, Alexander the Great, a powerful historical force, arrived in Israel, looking for his next conquest. Israel had allied with the Persians previously, but they knew that they had little chance in staving off Alexander's attacks; therefore, they chose to entreat him. The gamble paid off. In exchange for taxes, loyalty, and allowing the Greek Army to assume security control of Judea, Alexander permitted the Jews a great deal of autonomy.

The Anshei Knesset Hagdola - the Jewish governing body comprised of 120 Rabbis, would continue to govern, and the Jews would run their local affairs as they saw fit. The public received the treaty with great fanfare, and Jewish males born the following year were named Alexander in a show of tremendous gratitude. However, with Alexander's sudden death a few short years later, the honeymoon between Judea and Greece would soon come to an abrupt end.

The Greek empire was now divided into two by Alexander's generals who disagreed on where their new northern and southern empires should reside, putting Israel right in the middle. This came to a head around 190 BCE when the Seleucid empire of the north decided to attack the Ptolemaic empire of the south. With King Antiochus III of the Seleucid Empire now in charge of Judea, things were about to reach a boiling point. First, Antiochus banned all major Jewish observances, including the Sabbath, circumcision, and Kosher dietary laws on pain of death. He then passed a new edict that every Jewish bride could not get married until the local governor had his way with her. Lastly, he took over the Temple in Jerusalem and instituted Pagan worship. To make matters worse, some Jews, known as the Hellenists, went along with these decrees, generating massive anger within Jewish society.

In 166 BCE, two events would push a frustrated and angry Jewish public into full-blown revolt.

In the hills west of Jerusalem sits a town called Modi'in. The town has been rebuilt in modern times as a testament to Jewish continuity in the land. The mayor ordered the people to gather in the town square to make a public sacrifice to Zeus. He then further demanded that Matisyahu, the ousted High Priest of Jerusalem, make the offer to Zeus on behalf of the town. An outraged Matisyahu rose up and attacked instead, stabbing the mayor to death. The Greek troops tried to respond, but they were quickly surrounded and lynched by the angry townsmen.

Fearing retaliation and a repeat of this incident, Matisyahu encouraged all God-Fearing Jews to leave the towns and villages throughout Judea and go into hiding in the wilderness.

From the safety of caves, far away from the prying eyes of the Greeks and their Hellenist Jewish informers, they would be able to keep the laws of their religion in peace. Jews across the country took his advice, but the solution would not last long.

One Sabbath day, the authorities tracked down over 1000 Jews who had fled to worship in the wilderness. After warning them to come out and return to their homes, they refused. Greek troops stormed the caves, slaughtering all men, women, and children, and sending shockwaves throughout the county.

When word reached Matisyahu and his family, they decided enough was enough. He declared, "Whosoever shall come to make battle with us on the Sabbath day, we will fight against him; neither will we die all, as our brethren that were murdered in the secret places." (Book of Maccabees 1:2) Matisyahu and his family who were the progenitors of the Hasmoneans, a family of nobility and High Priests, would make their mark in history. The Jewish Revolt would now go into high gear.

Matisyahu's five sons quickly gathered together an army and decided upon guerilla tactics, using the caves nearby to hide in, and with their leadership, persuading nearly 12,000 men to join them.

Led by Matisyahu's son, Judah, they became known as the Maccabees which in Aramaic means "the hammer." It is also in reference to the first four letters of Exodus 15:11 in which Moses declared "Who is like you, God?" when the Israelites were saved by God from the Egyptians.

While the Maccabees eventually had almost 12,000 men, the Greek army brought nearly 50,000 into Judea. Using a hit and run method, the Maccabees were able to whittle down the army and force it to flee on numerous occasions. However, the campaign was not without cost. Out of the five sons that led the Maccabees, only one - Simon - lived.

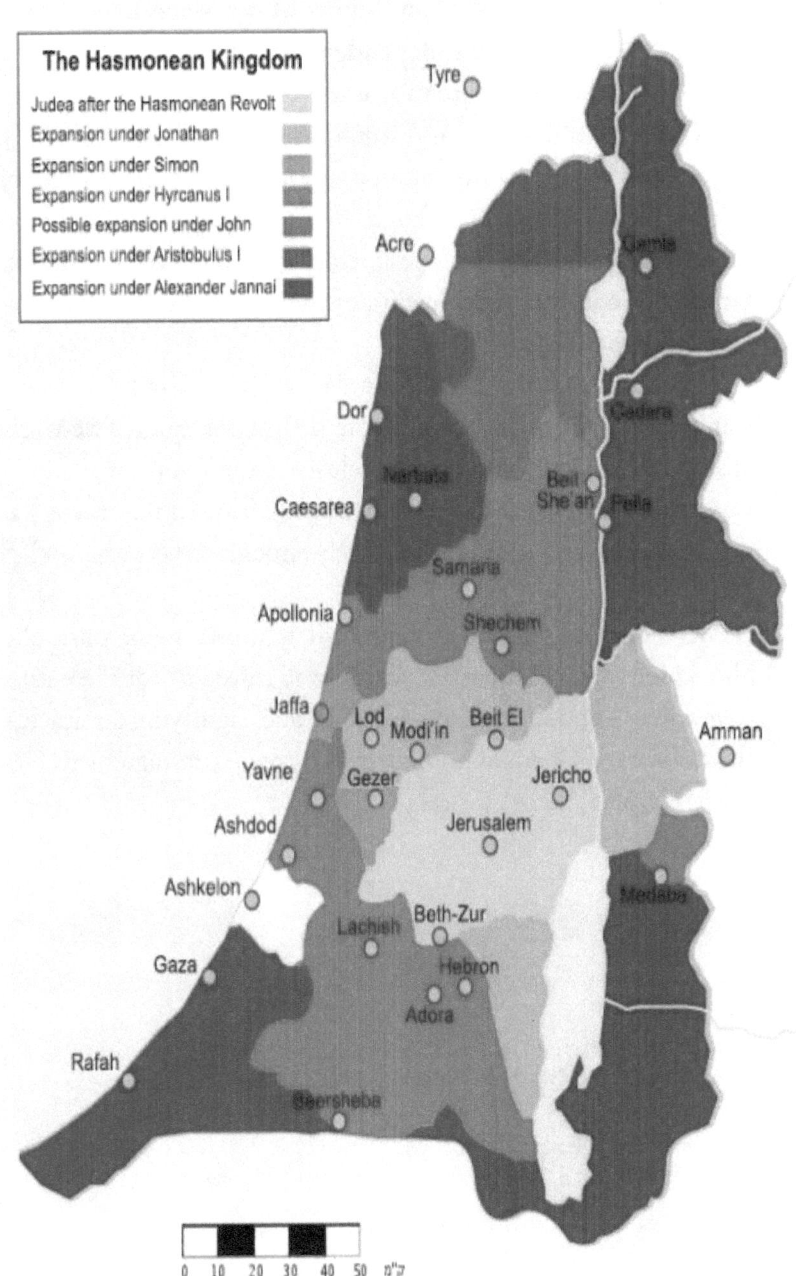
The Hasmonean Kingdom
Judea after the Hasmonean Revolt
Expansion under Jonathan
Expansion under Simon
Expansion under Hyrcanus I
Possible expansion under John
Expansion under Aristobulus I
Expansion under Alexander Jannai
Tyre
Acre
Gamla
Dor
Qedem
Narbata
Beit She'an
Pella
Caesarea
Samaria
Apollonia
Shechem
Jaffa
Lod
Modi'in
Beit El
Amman
Yavne
Gezer
Jericho
Ashdod
Jerusalem
Ashkelon
Medaba
Beth-Zur
Lachish
Gaza
Hebron
Adora
Rafah
Beersheba
0 10 20 30 40 50 ק"מ

The Hasmonean Empire of the Maccabees
Fully Independent 140-37BCE
Vassal State to Rome 37BCE-63CE (4)

The Maccabees' victory would reverberate throughout Jewish history, less because of their military prowess and more because of their spiritual revolt achieved through military means. One of the primary objectives of the war was the liberation of the Temple Mount from Greek rule and the re-dedication of the Temple to the worship of the One Almighty God.

According to the Torah, the Menorah required (or must be lit using) only pure olive oil with the seal of the High Priest. The seal ensured that the oil was created exclusively for Temple worship.

After clearing out the temple, they discovered that there was only one small jar left with the seal - barely enough to keep the wicks lit for a day.

It would take at least eight days to make more pure olive oil. Shockingly, after lighting the wicks, they stayed lit for the entire eight days when it should have gone out in one, signifying a miracle. Thus, the holiday of Chanukah lasts eight nights - a testament to God and the Maccabees' heroic efforts.

Exact Reproduction of the Menorah Commissioned by the Temple Institute of Jerusalem Awaiting to Be Lit in the 3rd Holy Temple on the Temple Mount.

After the miracle at the temple, the war with the Greeks lasted several more years, which resulted in the death of all of Simon's brothers. Simon, known to be a noble and holy person, became King and High Priest of Israel and ushered in what would become known as the Hasmonean era. During this era, Simon worked well with the Sanhedrin (the High Rabbinic Court), allowing them to handle religious teachings and conflicts, and he made an alliance with the Romans to counter the Greeks. Unfortunately, he was later killed by his son-in-law, who was persuaded to betray him by the Greeks. His son-in-law, John Hyrcanus, took over the throne and sided with a growing religious minority known as the Sadducees - a sect made up of upper-class Jews that aligned customs with Greek philosophies. They would come to oppose the Pharisees, who were traditional in their beliefs and followed the Torah.

Due to the Sadducees' rejection of the Oral Law, the very Oral Law that the Maccabees went to war to preserve, the decision of John Hyrcanus would prove disastrous and be the root of future civil unrest amongst the Jewish people. The Sadducees would persuade John that the Pharisees did not think he should be King and that his lineage was in question. According to the Talmud, this came to a head when at a banquet, where he was accused of not having the proper nobility to be King. Although his mother was cleared and he was found to be rightfully on the throne, he heeded the words of the Sadducees ever since.

The Sadducees would continue to dominate the Hasmonean line. During the festival of Sukkot, when hundreds of thousands of Jews traveled to Jerusalem to celebrate, Alexander Jannaeus, the sitting King and descendant of the Hasmonean dynasty, enacted the festive water libation ritual as a Sadducee would. Instead of pouring the water on the alter, as per the instruction of the Oral Law, Alexander poured it on his feet.

The dominantly pharisaic crowd booed and pelted Alexander with citron fruit used as part of the holiday's religious observance. In response, he had 6,000 Jews murdered that day by his soldiers and numerous Rabbis arrested and executed via crucifix - a Roman tradition. He would have men crucified as their women and children were killed in front of them.

In retaliation, the Pharisees enlisted a leader of the Syrian Greeks to assist, but the battle did not go as expected. The Jewish masses were not in the mood for civil war, and they did not want to fight against their brethren. Soon, the fighting simply dissipated. A peace was called via compromise, and it was decided that Alexander would govern while the Pharisees handled religious affairs. For a brief period, the Jewish Kingdom continued to grow, and Jews were even settled in Gaza in 96 BCE. Its Jewish community would last until it was destroyed in 1929 by the local Arabs, who coincidentally were mostly Egyptian.

The sons of Queen Salome and Alexander Janneus would fight against each other after their father's death and tensions surmounted even further after the death of the Queen.

Rome at this time was ruled by Pompey (who called himself Pompey the Great), a general who decided that Judea could not be allowed to remain neutral since it still divided the northern empire of Syria and the southern empire of Egypt. With the impressive history of the Maccabees preceding them, Pompey tried to conquer the Jews without fighting, using the civil war between the Jews to his advantage.

Pompey was able to defeat both sides and cause their surrender in months, and approximately 12,000 Jews were killed while trying to prevent him from entering the Temple.

Though Pompey would allow the Jews to keep the Temple and Hyrcanus as High Priest, he made sure to make his presence known, imposing taxes that heavily crippled their economy.

When Pompey went back to Rome, he thought he was going to be made Emperor, but Julius Caesar also wanted the job. Behind the scenes, Julius Caesar enlisted Hyrcanus to help him and the bet paid off. When Julius Caesar won the conflict between him and Pompey, he removed the taxes and laws that Pompey had placed upon the Jewish people; however, Hyrcanus, who had enjoyed some provisions under Pompey, was now denied the position of King over Israel and stripped of a great deal of power. Julius Caesar allowed the power to instead be given to Antipater, a gentile that served as the general for Hyrcanus' military.

This was the beginning of the end for his reign as he was eventually defeated by Herod (son of Antipater) and executed, resulting in the start of Roman rule over the Jews. Herod was a cruel ruler and essentially the end of the Hasmonean line. He married the granddaughter of Hyrcanus, but she did not love him back. Enraged, he had her grandfather and mother executed. When this did not convince her to requite his love, he executed her and their two sons.

After the sons were killed, there were no more living descendants of the Hasmoneans. The Talmud even declares in Kiddushin 70b that "anyone who claims to be from the House of the Hasmoneans is really descended from non-Jewish slaves." For all intents and purposes, the Hasmonean dynasty was now over.

Chapter 4 - The Death Throes of Jewish Autonomy

During the Herodian era, Rome began to grow in influence and power, but not everyone was satisfied with the status quo. There was a lot of unrest due to the class system created between the Pharisees and the Seleucids, causing the Jews to feel suffocated under the heavy Roman taxes and regulations. Much of the products and profits in the Jerusalem markets were given to the upper echelon of Roman society.

Herod was also a tyrant, establishing a police force that would murder anyone who thought of betraying him and killing everyone who voiced opinions against him, even if they were from his own family line. However, much of present-day Israel does boast sites that were erected by Herod, including Sabaste in the Hills of Ephraim, many fortresses, and an expanded Temple Mount Plaza.

The total renovation of the Second Temple began in 19 BCE and was completed nearly 50 years later. Herod doubled the size of the Temple Mount plaza and turned the Temple itself into one of the most magnificent buildings of his time. "Whoever has not seen Herod's Temple has not seen a beautiful building in his life," declared the Rabbis. (Bava Batra 4a.) The most famous retaining wall of the Mount, the Western Wall, still stands today at about four to five stories high. During Herod's time, it cleared 12 stories.

Jewish Worshippers Prostrate in Prayer on Their Holy Temple Mount. Due to Concerns over International Condemnation and Arab Violence, the Israeli Police Currently Only Permit Jewish Prayer on a Secluded Path along the Eastern Wall of the Mount, Several Hours a Day, 5 days a Week.

**Jews Gather for Prayer at the Western Wall of the Temple Mount
on the Holiday of Sukkot.**

The Hasmonean Dynasty was clearly over once Herod died. No matter what he tried to do with marriage, once his son, Archelaus, took over the throne, the Jews rejected him and nearly caused another rebellion. The Romans did not like the possibility of a rebellion, given the Jews fierce fighting record, so they had Herod's son poisoned.

Herod's grandson, Agrippas, would ascend and become the last King of the Jews. It is said that religion and government were united under his rule. When Caligula, emperor of Rome, wanted his statue placed in the Temple of Jerusalem to be worshipped, Agrippas quickly argued with Caligula, explaining how this could ignite a rebellion (especially since this very act is what resulted in the rise of the Hasmoneans). Caligula surprisingly listened, and the only place in all of Rome where his statue was not erected was in Jerusalem. Once again, this is a testament to the great significance that the Jewish people place on their homeland and their spiritual monuments and landmarks.

Agrippas ensured that the Jews were able to practice their traditions, and he tried to ensure that they were not heavily taxed by Rome. He befriended many Rabbis, and was generally loved by the people. A testament of his worth is accounted in Sotah 41a of the Talmud in which every seven years, the King would read the book of Deuteronomy to the people. When he came to Deuteronomy 17:15, he cried, because the verse said that the Jews should not have a King who is a foreigner, and he was one. The Rabbis told him, "Do not fear, Agrippas. You are our brother." Though this went against Jewish tradition and laws to make such statements, it speaks to his influence and reputation as King.

With his sudden death in 44 CE, the stability felt throughout his rule would quickly come to an end.

The Jewish people were divided into the Sicarii—who wanted Rome out of the country, the Sadducees, early Christians, and the Pharisees. This was further exacerbated by the heir to the throne, Agrippa II, who was the great-grandson of Agrippa. Unlike his great grandfather, he did not care for the Jewish religion and preferred the Roman way of life, often using soldiers and military governors to enforce his rule.

Anti-Jewish sentiment soon began to rise through two major figures. The first was a Greek named Apion, who wrote about how Jews were cheaters and drank the blood of others. The second was Cicero, the Roman orator who spoke negatively against the Jews. Their words kindled the growing hate for Jews in Roman society.

Chapter 5 - Judea Takes a Final Stand

In 66 CE, Jewish frustration with Rome boiled over into an outright rebellion. It was led by Yosef ben Mattityahu Hakohen (also known by his roman name, historian Josephus Flavius). The catalyst of this rebellion was a group of Greeks who sacrificed in front of the central synagogue of Caesarea on the Sabbath as a means of provocation. The Jews tried to first appeal to the Roman Governor Gessius Florus via a delegation of dignitaries, but he not only rejected their plea, but even arrested the Jewish delegates! The Jewish community responded in a fury. In retaliation, the Holy Temple was raided and statues of Emperor Nero and Gessius Flora were erected. Gessius Flora would continue to demand that the Jews follow polytheism and the Jews could not take it anymore – it was war.

The Romans enlisted their head general, Vespasian, to quell the rebellion. Heading to the Galilee, they killed civilians and military men alike while setting entire towns ablaze. Approximately 10,000 Jews were murdered or sold into slavery. In the summer of 70 CE, Roman soldiers broke through the walls of Jerusalem after a four-month siege. After a fierce three-week battle in the city, the Holy Temple was set on fire on the 9th Day of the Hebrew month of Av, the same date the first Temple was destroyed nearly 600 years earlier by Babylon. To this very day, this day of destruction is observed as a National Day of Jewish mourning, marked by fasting, sitting on low stools, and refraining from any manifestations of joy like washing, music or even wearing leather shoes, observed from sunset to sunset. As the Temple went up in flames, so did the role of the priestly class - the burden of Jewish continuity now fell squarely on the shoulders of the Rabbis.

According to the testimony of Josephus, over 1 million Jews were killed, with approximately 70,000 Jews enslaved to build the Roman Coliseum. The treasures and holy artifacts of the Temple were marched to Rome in a grand victory march, a scene from which can still be seen on the Arch of Titus in Rome till this very day.

The Arch of Titus in Rome - The Destruction of Judea Forever Etched in Stone. (5)

Chapter 6 Bar Kochva: Has the Messiah Arrived?

The next and last major Jewish rebellion was the Bar-Kochhba Revolt from 132-135 CE. The Roman emperor, Hadrian, enacted a wide number of anti-Jewish decrees echoing those that sparked the uprising of the Maccabees just 300 years prior. While the sight of the destroyed Temple greatly distressed the Jews, Hadrian's order for the construction of a Roman Temple over the ruins would be a pill too bitter to swallow. The public was ripe for a renewed revolt. Anticipating a growing conflict, the Jews began crafting weapons and setting up camps in nearby caves to prepare for a rebellion.

In 123 C.E, they started their guerilla warfare. Hadrian sent an army to squash the rebellion, and fighting continued for years until Hadrian left Judea in 132 C.E. The Jews escalated their attacks. Shimon Bar-Kochhba, the leader of the rebellion, led the Jews into taking over nearly 50 strongholds and nearly 1000 towns and villages. Jews from other countries began joining the campaign. The initial stage of the revolt was so successful that Rebbe Akiva, the most revered rabbi of the generation, declared Bar-Kochhba as the long-awaited Messiah, and even ordered his disciples to join the battle. Over 24,000 heeded his call. Additionally, preparations for rebuilding the Temple in Jerusalem began in earnest.

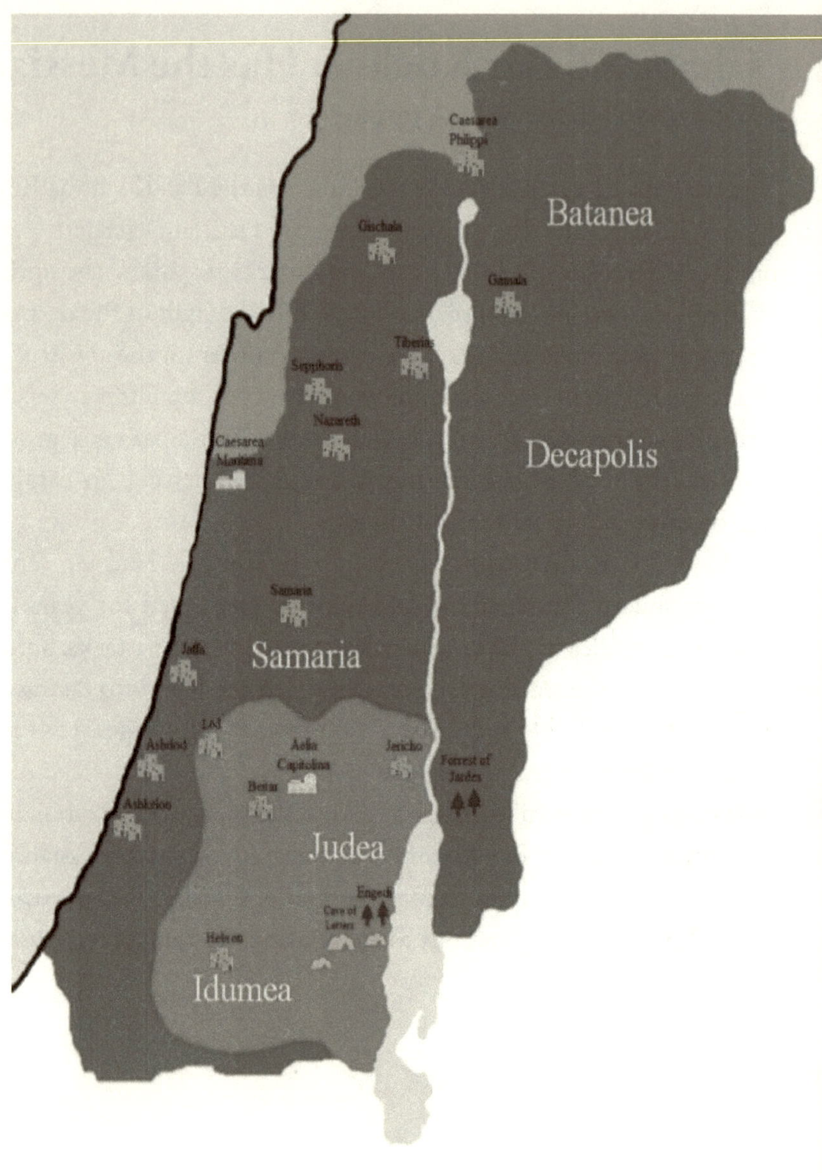
Caesarea Philippi
Batanea
Gischala
Gamala
Tiberias
Sepphoris
Nazareth
Decapolis
Caesarea Maritima
Samaria
Samaria
Jaffa
Lod
Ashdod
Aelia Capitolina
Jericho
Forrest of Jardes
Betar
Ashkelon
Judea
Engedi
Cave of Letters
Hebron
Idumea

The Short-Lived Bar Kochva Mini State Extended to the Areas Around Judea and Idumea. (6)

Bar Kochva Even Started to Reproduce the Shekel Currency That Had Been Used in the Previous Jewish Kingdoms. The Coin on the Left Features an Image of the Temple, While the Right Coin Proclaims: "To the Freedom of Jerusalem." (Photo Credit: Classical Numismatic Group, Inc.)

However, the tides turned when Hadrian sent General Julius Severus, along with twelve other armies from various countries (such as Egypt, Britain, Syria, and more) aligned against the Jews. Severus would not engage directly, instead taking over the Jew's supply routes and fortresses, stopping the halt of resources and food until they grew weak. Then he would strike. The Romans destroyed all of the fortresses and villages that the Jews had taken. The final battle at Bethar, Bar-Kochhba's base of operations, was on a mountainside overlooking a valley, but it did not withstand Hadrian's army. The walls of Bethar fell and every Jew there was murdered.

Over half a million Jews were slaughtered, and many survivors were sold into slavery and sent to Egypt. In anger, Hadrian put forth several decrees that related to the Jews, including forbidding them from engaging with the Torah, circumcision, from observing the Sabbath, holding Jewish courts, congregating in synagogues and practicing their traditions. This essentially denied the Jews everything that defined their religion and traditions.

Jerusalem became a pagan city known as Aelia Capitolina and Jews were not allowed to set foot there on pain of death. Entry would be permitted only one day a year, on the 9th of Av, to allow Jews to mourn their own destruction The ban would last for almost 200 years until the Byzantines took over. Judea's name was changed to Syria Palestina, a name that would remain for the next 1825 years. For nearly two millennia, a remaining tiny Jewish minority would watch as powerful nations would come and go, praying for their redemption and the promised ingathering of their exiled brethren.

Chapter 7: A Land in Desolation Weeps for Her Children

נחם ה' אלהינו את אבלי ציון ואת אבלי ירושלים, ואת העיר האבלה והחרבה והבזויה והשוממה. האבלה מבלי בניה, והחריבה ממעונותיה, והבזויה מכבודה, והשוממה מאין יושב.

"Console, Lord our God, the mourners of Zion and the mourners of Jerusalem, and the city that is in mourning and ruins, despised and desolate. Mourning because she is bereft of her children, ruined of her dwellings, despised in contrast to her former glory, desolate without inhabitants."

Prayer recited on the 9th of Av - Day of Judea's Destruction

Around 325 CE, the emperor Constantine, decreed that Christianity was to be the ruling religion of Rome. Since Christians began to view Jerusalem as holy, due to its association to Jesus, Constantine also began to restore the city. However, he was no ally to the Jews.

After moving the capital from Rome to Constantinople, he warned Jews that they were not to interfere with anyone who wanted to convert to Christianity. He also made it a crime to become a Jew and there was a ban on marriage between Jews and Christians. Jews otherwise were able to maintain their identity and religious practices. Still, the movement of the capital created a way for Christianity to spread faster while Judaism was forbidden to expand outside of its tight communal confines.

In 351 C.E, the Jews revolted against Gallus who attempted to place more sanctions and regulations upon them. As a result, all of the major cities in Galilee were razed and destroyed.

The Jewish people also faced great uncertainty in the face of Rome's crumbling empire as it had already split into two Kingdoms. The Western and Eastern Kingdoms were at war, suffering from inflation and facing constant threats from other nations attempting to overthrow them.

In 363 CE, the new Emperor of the Eastern Kingdom, Julian the Apostate was somewhat of an ally to the Jews and even allowed them to rebuild the Temple in Jerusalem, however, not long after the project began, he died in battle in 363, putting a halt to those plans. In 476 C.E, the Western Kingdom was taken over by what the Romans called the Barbarians. The Eastern Kingdom, also known as Byzantine was able to fend of various armies, keeping Judea intact.

Meanwhile, the "Barbarians" became Christians and maintained a harsh rule in the Western Kingdom, enacting policies that would affect Jews for generations to come. For example, when Emperor Theodosius took over in the fifth century, he ordered that Jews should be persecuted because of their involvement in the crucifixion of Jesus. They were prevented from building new places of worship, forbidden to own slaves, given harsher taxes, could not take on government roles, and Jews could not preside over court cases between Jews and non-Jews, making justice difficult. Conversion to Judaism was a crime, and marriage between a Jew and non-Jew was forbidden. It is a miracle that the Jewish people were able to thrive under such stringent laws as the only role that they were able to play publicly was that of the despised tax collector.

Basically, the Jews were able to practice their religion within their own communities but they were not able to introduce it or try to convert others. This allowed the emperor to maintain his stance that religion was not to be interfered with while simultaneously ensuring a decline in the Jewish population. Later, John Chrysostom in Antioch would give several public sermons in which he preached Jews to be the root of all evil. These sermons further fueled anti-Jewish sentiments based in Christian writings, which depicted Jews—and Pharisees in particular—in a highly unfavorable light. The flames of antisemitism were about to rage out of control.

In the 6th Century, Emperor Justinian I brought even harsher sentiments as he tried to change Jewish traditions and force them to become more in line with Christianity. One notable instance was when he made it forbidden for them to use the Mishna which was used to help them interpret the Torah. Instead, he gave them texts that they were told to use for interpretation and forbade them from reading in Hebrew. Wisely, Jewish scholars wrote supplemental material that referred to the Mishna, and because this material was not the Mishna itself, it was not banned, and therefore they were able to get around this particular law.

The synagogues became churches and he ordered the destruction of all non-Christian places of worship throughout northern Africa. Jews were seen as pagans, not serving the true Christian god. They weren't even able to testify against Christians in court, regardless of what was done to them, causing the Jews to be seen as lower class as the years went on.

Easter, a budding Christian holiday, was placed over Passover, which meant that by law, Jews were not able to practice Passover on the proper day and had to wait. As a result, Passover observance went underground, with Jews practicing in secret.

He would eventually try to get rid of Judaism altogether, but as one may deduce by now, the Jews do not respond well to having their religion outlawed or altered. Riots broke out and continued until a new emperor, Heracilus, took power. The Jews successfully aligned with the Persians and even retook Jerusalem. However, the victory was short-lived as Heracilus soon recaptured the city with his army, punishing the Jews by slaughtering many and forcing others to convert to Christianity. This forced conversion continued well into the 12th century, with non-Christians given the ultimatum to either convert or face death. Many Jews chose martyrdom rather than renounce their faith.

The Jewish people were able to survive four crusades by the Byzantine empire though it was not without heavy losses. As the Byzantine empire began to fracture, many anti-Jewish laws were not enacted or ignored allowing them to live relatively peacefully and maintain their traditions. In desperate times, the Jews were seen as a resource. For example, Theodore Doukas, emperor of Epiros, did nothing to the Jews until five years after his coronation, but then he confiscated their property to help finance his government.

John Vatatzes, emperor of Nicaea, continued the campaign of persecution by forcing Jews to convert to Christianity or face death. Michael VIII Palaiologos took the throne while seeking a shifty alliance, asking the Jews to support him in exchange for not being forced to convert to Christianity. Still, this arrangement did not last upon his death. With new leadership taking power, the Jews once again faced the harsh reality of choosing between denying their faith or risking their lives.

Eventually, the Jewish people attempted to join with the encroaching Sasanian Empire that attempted to overtake the Byzantine Empire. It is estimated that at least 10% of the Jewish population joined in the revolt against the Byzantine Empire. Led by Nehemiah ben Hushiel (the revolution's leader) and Benjamin of Tiberias (a wealthy man that was able to help fund the effort), there was even an attempt to reconquer Jerusalem.

After a relatively easy takeover, Nehemiah ben Hushiel became the ruler of Jerusalem and began making plans to usher in a new High Priesthood and a new Temple. However, he was killed only a few months later in a Christian counterattack. Though both sides would gain and lose the upper hand in an ongoing back and forth, the power balance shifted when the Persians allied with the Christians in 617 C.E. Matters were further complicated when Emperor Heraclius of the Byzantine Empire sought to take over lands ruled by the Sasanian Empire, including Jerusalem. Benjamin of Tiberias and his men surrendered and asked for an alliance to which Heraclius would later go back on. Jews were banned from living within three miles of Jerusalem and massacres across the country soon followed. Many fled to Egypt for safety.

Despite Heraclius' conquest, the Arab Caliphates would soon come to rule the holy land. By 640, the Islamic military had taken over most of Syria, Mesopotamia and Syria Palestina. Though the current ruler, Umar, established a pact that would protect Jews from death and not require them to convert to Islam, they were still decreed as inferior. Nothing, however, would prepare both religious groups for the future Crusades.

The year that Pope Urban II began the crusades, a campaign to free Jerusalem from the "infidels" began, lasting over 200 years. Over 60,000 people signed up for the mission, pillaging the lands between them and Jerusalem and killing anyone that went against their cause. In 1099, the knights of the First Crusade captured Jerusalem. The Jewish community was burned to death or sold into slavery. Later, others were thrown into water and forcibly baptized. Those who refused were killed. Many Jews who "accepted baptism" continued practicing Judaism in the shadows, while European countries persisted in their efforts to forcibly convert all non-Christians, with a particular focus on the Jews, whom they labeled 'Christ-killers.'

There was a brief respite for the Jews during the reign of the Ayyubids and Mamluk Sultanates. The Ayyubids were a dynasty of sultans that were known for their military prowess, including taking over Jerusalem in 1187 and conquering parts of Egypt, Yemen, and East Asia. Saladin Yusuf, founder of the Ayyubid dynasty, allowed the Jews to return to Jerusalem and the Jewish population grew under his leadership. Later, Saladin divided the conquered territories and gave them to his sons who kept conflicts relatively low between them. Eventually, they were forced to unite against the Crusaders after their father's death. The Ayyubid dynasty later came to an end after the bloodline was severed and subsequently taken over by the Mamluks - a military group comprised of former Egyptian slaves that practiced the Muslim faith.

Under Mamluk rule, there was disagreement on what to do with the "dhimmis" or what was referred to as the "protected people - Christian and Jews." Part of this was due to their disdain against Christianity for the over two centuries of Crusade fighting they had endured. However, because of this, Jews were seen as "potential allies, diplomats, and spies."

This complex relationship with the Mamluks highlights the broader historical context of Jewish survival in the region. Among the Jewish community's closest relatives are the Samaritans, who are the last known remnant of three of the ten Israelite tribes (Efrayim, Menashe, and Levi) who resided in the northern Kingdom of Israel during the

First Temple period. Despite all of the wars and displacements of the Jewish people, they never left the area of Shechem (where the tomb of their forefather, the prophet Joseph, lies). As blood brothers of the Jews and practitioners of Torah law (albeit with some key disagreements with the Jews - chiefly Jerusalem vs Mount Gerizim as the Holy City), they are a testament to the history of the Jewish people in the land. Today the Samaritans' numbers have dwindled significantly, numbering just 700 souls in all.

Yitzhaq II ben Amram ben Shalma ben Tabia - The Samaritan High Priest from 1916-32. (7)

Modern Samaritans— The Last Remnants of the Kingdom of Israel, Worship on Mount Gerizim—Their Holiest Site. (8)

Although the government implemented a color identification system in which Christians had to wear blue turbans, Jews had to wear yellow, and Samaritans had to wear red, it is generally accepted that Jewish faith and culture was better off under this period than under the time of the Crusades—a time in which violence and death was a constant threat. The Ottomans would be the ones to end the reign of the Mamluks around 1516.

The Ottoman Empire afforded the Jewish people a sense of communal dignity, that many of their past rulers in recent centuries had denied them. For example, Sultan Bayezid II declared that the Ottoman Empire was "not to refuse the Jews entry or cause them difficulties, but to receive them cordially." After the Mamluks were defeated, European Jews were encouraged to escape persecution and find homes within the Ottoman Empire. Without extreme persecution, the Jews were able to take on positions as physicians, bring the printing press to the Ottoman Empire, and thus literature, education and economic opportunities flourished as a result.

Meanwhile, the situation in Palestine was one of neglect and decay. The famed 17th-century French author and explorer, Jean Doubdan, in Le Voyage de la Terre-Sainte, described the central road between Jerusalem and Gaza as a terrain "rugged and difficult, filled with thorny bushes and large stones, making travel extremely challenging, even for horses." By the 1700s the situation remained unchanged when Thomas Shaw, a British archaeologist observed that Palestine didn't have enough population to farm the land. Later in the eighteenth century, Count Constantine Frangois Volney, a French historian, detailed in his writings that Palestine was "ruined and desolate... the traveler meets nothing but houses in ruins, cisterns rendered useless, and fields abandoned..."

As late as 1862, even ancient towns and holy sites across the land were in a state of truncation and dilapidation, highlighted through these photos from the From the Library of Congress.

The Old City of Hebron

The Old City of Gaza

The Old City of Shechem (Nablus)

Grass Grows between the Stones of the Dilapidated and Deserted Temple Mount - 1862 (Francis Bedford)

The prolonged disregard in Palestine took its toll. As agriculture and infrastructure degraded, population growth stagnated and even declined. In fact, around 1900, less than 100,000 people resided in what is now called 'the West Bank,' with a significant Jewish population. Even as late as 1951, the 'native' (Arab) population of Gaza numbered only 80,000. (UNRWA report 1951-1952)

To grasp the shifts during this time, one must also consider the social obstacles they faced.

In Willam B. Ziff's 1938 book, he writes,

It was always the foreign soldier who was the police power in Palestine. The Tulunides brought in Turks and Negroes. The Fatamids introduced Berbers, Slavs, Greeks, Kurds, and mercenaries of all kinds. The Mamelukes imported legions of Georgians and Circassians. Each monarch for his personal safety relied on great levies of slave warriors. Saladin, hard-pressed by the Crusaders, received one hundred and fifty thousand Persians who were given lands in Galilee and the Sidon district for their services.

Out of this human patch-work of Jews, Arabs, Armenians, Kalmucks, Persians, Crusaders, Tartars, Indians, Ethiopians, Egyptians, Sudanese, Turks, Mongols, Romans, Kharmazians, Greeks, pilgrims, wanderers, ne'er-do-wells and adventurers, invaders, slaves ... was formed that hodge-podge of blood and mentality we call today "Levantine." ...

Many historians and authors agree that the sudden surge in the Arab population during the mandate could not possibly be due to "natural growth," and the account is clear:

Though the government solemnly estimates in 1937 a total Moslem increase by immigration of only 22,535 since the time of the British occupation, evidence of a vast influx of desert tribesmen is obvious everywhere. As early as 1926, Colonial Secretary Amery cautiously conceded that despite the growth of the Jewish element "the increase of the Arabs is actually greater than the Jews." Figures presented before the Peel Commission in 1937 showed the Arab population to have more than doubled in fourteen years. This admitted gain in half a generation must either be attributed to outside immigration or to the most astonishing philo-progenitiveness in medical history. ...

[T]he government itself acknowledged in 1922 the immigration of whole tribes "from the Hejaz and southern Transjordan into the Beersheba area," a fact which in itself must make its estimates of Arab immigration far-fetched. Other approximate figures are available from scattered but credible sources. One of these is the statement of the French governor of the Hauran in Syria, that from his district alone, in the summer of 1933, thirty-five thousand people had left for Palestine as a consequence of bad crops.

These accounts of a relatively barren land were common, and it was not until around the 19th century that antisemitism arose greatly and thoughts began to change. Around this time, nationalism was on the rise. Much of this was due to the influence of Christian Arabs who brought along their beliefs that Jews had a hand in the crucifixion of Jesus. Growing conflicts resulted in massacres of Jews in Baghdad in 1828 and Barfurush in 1867.

In the "Damascus Affair," several Jews were arrested after being blamed for the murder of Father Thomas, a Christian. They were tortured to the point of confession even though there was no evidence of their involvement. Antisemitism continued to grow until the Ottomon Empire was taken over by European countries in the early twentieth century, which put the Jews under Christian rule.

In the early twentieth century, the League of Nations created a mandate in which an international power could oversee non-governed regions, ensuring the survival and future success of that region's population. Many regions were given to different countries to oversee and carefully consider how that region should be mandated. On July 24, 1922, the region known as Palestine was given to Great Britain. Great Britian evaluated the historical significance of the area via committee, analyzed the population and developed a course of action that would be best for its people.

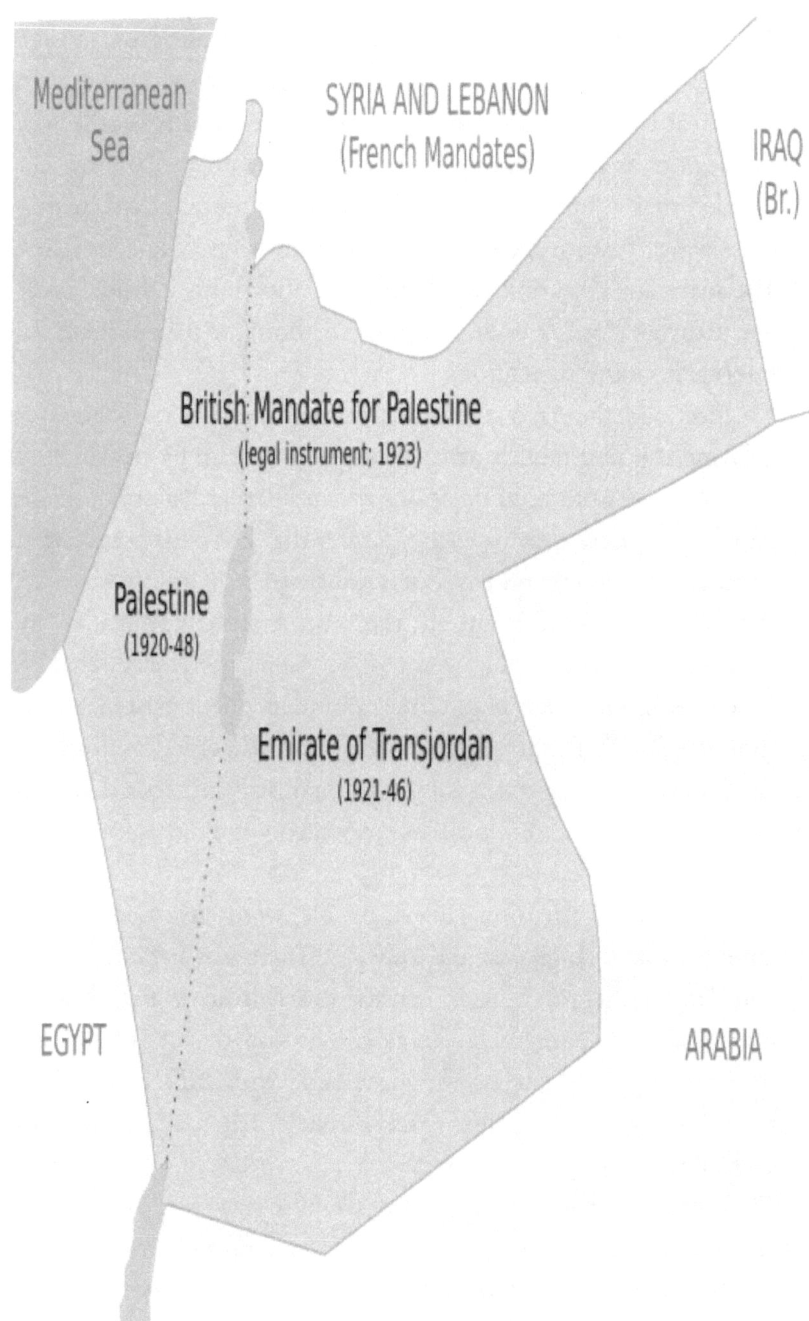

Mediterranean Sea
SYRIA AND LEBANON
(French Mandates)
IRAQ (Br.)
British Mandate for Palestine
(legal instrument; 1923)
Palestine
(1920-48)
Emirate of Transjordan
(1921-46)
EGYPT
ARABIA

British Mandate of Palestine: Note That the Mandate Covers Both Sides of the Jordan River. (9)

Great Britian could have easily denied the Jewish people access to the region, as it was under their authority to do so. However, they decided that a Jewish Homeland was to be re-established, seeing that there was a "historical connection of the Jewish people with Palestine." The mandate also took the Arab population into consideration and decided that both Jews and Arabs had the right to handle their own internal laws and regulations.

However, the Arab communities fought against the mandate, thus delaying the re-establishment of the Jewish State by nearly 30 years. Unlike the rest of the populations that resided in Palestine, the Jewish people were seen as the sole community that had a historical, spiritual, cultural, emotional and psychological tie to the land. It was said that the "most interesting of all the non-Arab communities in the country...is without a doubt the Samaritan sect in Nablus (Shechem)...which has maintained an independent existence from the time the Jewish People entered the land of Israel led by Joshua 3300 years ago." They split from the Jewish mainstream over a debate where the Temple should be located—Jerusalem or in their view, Mount Gerizim.

Meanwhile, the non-Jewish people were vast and spread out amongst many languages and cultures. There was little homogeneity, and "no authentic official census exists from which satisfactory information...is obtainable." In fact, it is said that it is "no easy task to write concisely and at the same time with sufficient fullness on the ethnology of Palestine." (Encyclopedia Britannica 11 ed. Vol. 20. 604-605).

History notes that there weren't even many inhabitants at all. According to the 2017 paper, *Local Malaria Elimination: A Historical Perspective from Palestine 100 Years Ago Informs the Current Way Forward in Sub-Saharan Africa*, Palestine, for several centuries before

World War I was "severely saturated in malaria...[making it] either uninhabitable in many areas or otherwise very thinly populated." Furthermore, the article breaks down how Palestinians were not a single culture and people as "several displaced Muslim communities from other parts of the Ottoman Empire...Algerians, and Bosnians, were periodically introduced and resettled by the Ottoman Empire into the region...there was no national identity and no cohesion between the inhabitants other than to their own religion, individual group, or tribe. There was no notion of a Palestinian entity or nation; the population was, as previously mentioned by Kligler in his 1930 textbook, 'of mixed peoples, many religions, and all gradations of civilization' who happened to be in Palestine at that moment." The British Commission of 1929 expounded upon the notion, admitting that "for the last six centuries, Palestine is an artificial conception...Its frontiers, too, are largely artificial."

What a stark difference from how the policies of the British Mandate related to the Jewish people!

Some of the Arab population in Palestine followed traditional laws and rules from Islam. Some did not. Some of the populations were comprised of nomads, and nearly half of the Arab population had arrived in Israel during the British mandate. This meant that large swaths of the Arab population had no history or past with the land before the early twentieth century, let alone an established culture.

Despite all of this, Palestinians are encouraged to keep fighting, to this very day. In a newspaper interview, Bir Zeit President Nasir stated that, "the destiny of the Arab College at Beir Zeit is to be the nucleus around which is built the Palestinian state." Students of even the most liberal of colleges see themselves as the "the future 'Palestine' leaders...and the PLO leaders of tomorrow."

This is concerning because as the late Rabbi Meir Kahane wrote in his book, *They Must Go:*

What inexplicable loss of national preservation, will, and sanity makes the Jews of Israel hesitate to save themselves? We know that the Arab believes that we are thieves who stole his land. We know that he murdered Jews in the land from the beginning of the Zionist revival and attempted to destroy the Jewish state at birth. We know that under the best of circumstances he is a defeated enemy who suffered a humiliating disaster that turned him from a majority in the land into a minority in a Jewish state ruled by the Jewish people and whose character and destiny are stated de jure as being Jewish. We know that the Arab differs from us in every possible way—ethnically, religiously, culturally, linguistically—and that everything about the Jewish state is foreign to him. We know that he grows explosively in quantity (even as Jews do not), and that in the face of his huge population growth and the pitiful Jewish birthrate, aliya figures, and abortions, he will be a powerful and dangerous minority tomorrow, aiming—under the democratic rights of the state—to be a majority in the future. We know that he is educated and ever more radical, and that his students and intellectuals openly call for support of the PLO and a "Palestine" state rather than Israel.

They fight for their land, yet there is nothing substantial to justify the fight. Within the region's borders, there are large groups of those from Armenia, Greece, Italy, Persia, Germany, Bosnia, Turkey, Sudan, Algeria and more, all with a mix of Christian and Muslim sects, and these are only those that have a permanent residence. As recent as 2012, the Hamas Minister of the Interior and of National Security, Fathi Hammad, made the following statement on Al-Hekma TV while asking for assistance from other Arabic nations:

"Brothers, half of the Palestinians are Egyptians and the other half are Saudis. Who are the Palestinians? We have many families called Al-Masri, whose roots are Egyptian. Egyptian! They may be from Alexandria, from Cairo, from Damietta, from the North, from Aswan, from Upper Egypt. We are Egyptians. We are Arabs. We are Muslims. We are a part of you."

Historically, the lack of cohesion held back progress and stunted the region. Instead of Kingdoms, inventions, and cultural advancements, the country remained bare and disorganized.

For example, communication in the country was conducted solely by caravan until 1892. Roads for carriages were barely maintained. There were no mines, and almost all of the country was comprised of agriculture. At that time, it was said that "Palestine is essentially a land of small divisions, and its configuration does not fit it to form a single entity. It has never belonged to one nation and probably never will." (Encyclopedia Britannica 11th Ed, vol 20. 604-605).

Is it any wonder then, why the mandate decided that the Israelites should be re-established there? To Great Britain, this was not a displacement of others, but a rightful inheritance granted back to the heirs.

Chapter 8 - The Arabs Resist the Return of the Jews

In 1917, the British Government made a public declaration known as "the Balfour Declaration," an open support for a "national home for the Jewish people." This declaration was negotiated between the British, Zionist Jews and even anti-Zionist Jews. The declaration took into account the current Arab population in the region, ensuring that there was never an effort to remove them from their homes. It was merely an affirmation of the historical birthright of the Jewish People to the land of their forefathers. This was significant because it was the first public support for Zionism by a major world superpower and it was immediately aligned with the British Mandate.

This is not to say there was not already a movement towards Zionism. The Russian Empire at the time had introduced several laws known as the May Laws, heavily regulating its Jewish citizens. They were forbidden to live outside of towns, unable to give land to other Jews, and they were forbidden to perform any type of business on Sundays and any other traditional Christian holidays. These laws resulted in anti-Jewish riots "called pogroms" and a mass exodus from Russia, resulting in over two million Jews leaving the country. With antisemitism on the rise, desire for an established homeland grew.

In 1897, the First Zionist Congress, led by its chairperson Theodor Herzl, stated that "Zionism seeks for the Jewish people a publicly recognized legally secured homeland in Palestine." In subsequent congresses, there was special care taken into securing financial backing towards the cause, creating a more formidable political presence, and ensuring that the culture of the Jewish people remained intact. Others in the congress suggested that a homeland be established in Uganda, but this was rejected when members considered the historical and spiritual significance of their homeland. In fact, in 1903, the British offered Herzl and the congress the option of an independent Jewish state in East Africa (known as the Uganda project). Serious thought was given to the possibility, but it was argued that no other area could replace Israel's original homeland. By the time the twelfth congress was in play, the British Mandate had become a reality.

Jewish Returnees to the Land Farm the Galilee at Kibbutz Degania in 1921. (10)

Under the British Mandate, accommodations were made to help Jewish exiles get back home, resulting in a significant spike in the Jewish population in "Palestine" from 9% to 27% between 1922 and 1935. However, in 1939, the British government attempted to change its mandate by limiting the number of returning exiles, planning to end immigration entirely by 1944 without Arab consent. This policy was dubbed the "White Paper." These changes were due to extreme violence by Palestinian Arabs who were vehemently against the mandate from the start.

The Jewish Agency for Palestine was swift in their reaction, stating that the White Paper placed a "territorial ghetto for Jews in their own homeland...[the] policy [is] a breach of faith and a surrender to Arab terrorism." The Jews claimed that they that had no animus against the Arab people but "the Arabs are not landless or homeless as are the Jews. They are not in need of emigration. Jewish colonization has benefited Palestine and all its inhabitants...[including] the liberation of the Arab peoples." The Jewish people, in historic fashion, decided to fight and raise their concerns rather than succumb to this injustice.

Rabbi Yitzhak Herzog, who would become the first Chief Rabbi of Israel would go on to say, "We cannot agree to the White Paper. Just as the prophets did before me, I hereby rip it in two," to which he ripped it apart publicly.

When World War II erupted later that year, the changes were put on hold. However, on the day that the British Mandate expired in 1948, the Jewish People's Council at the Tel Aviv Museum declared into existence the State of Israel, with a declaration of independence having been written two weeks prior. The need for the Jewish people to have a home and declare their independence became even more apparent after the wholesale destruction of European Jewry in the Holocaust.

In the declaration read that day, it states, "The catastrophe which recently befell the Jewish people - the massacre of millions of Jews in Europe - was another clear demonstration of the urgency of solving the problem of its homelessness by re-establishing in Eretz-Israel the Jewish State, which would open the gates of the homeland wide to every Jew and confer upon the Jewish people the status of a fully privileged member of the community of nations."

It only took four hours for Egypt to bomb Tel Aviv.

The Jewish People Declare Renewed Independence after 1,878 years of Exile on May 14, 1948. Ben Gurion, Israel's First Prime Minister, Stands at Center Stage. (11)

Even after the Balfour Declaration was first issued, the Arabs living in Palestine were against a shared home. They claimed the Jews had no right to the land even though they themselves had no claim. The Palestine Arab Congress in 1919 even stated that "our district Southern Syria or Palestine should be not separated from the Independent Arab Syrian Government and be free from all foreign influence and protection." They later met with the Syrian National Congress to "inform Arab patriots there of the decision to call Palestine Southern Syria and unite it with northern Syria." Though this decision did not pan out, it begs the question, if Palestine were a people and state in of itself, why would they be considered Southern Syria?

There was even a banner being flown during a demonstration in Jerusalem that year reading, "Palestine is part of Syria." Demonstrators even demanded that Palestine become Southern Syria.

1919 Arab Demonstration in Jerusalem. The Banners Read: "Palestine is Southern Syria" (12)

Meanwhile, the British tried to set up a majority Arab population by simultaneously halting Jewish immigration and turning a blind eye to the Arab influx. According to official British records they "requested the French to stop monitoring illegal Arab immigration along the border of Lebanon and Syria with West Palestine (Israel) allowing free immigration of Arabs into Western Palestine (Israel)."

In 1920, mass Arab unrest broke out in what would become known as the 1920 Nebi Musa riots, resulting in the deaths of five Jews and hundreds more injured. Leading up to this event, the Jewish people expressed concerns over security matters because of rising tensions and the death of Joseph Trumpeldor at the battle in Tel Hai. He was well-known for creating He-Halutz, an organization that prepared the youth for "settlement in Eretz-Israel," and he was an early Zionist hero that fought for his country.

These worries came to fruition when the riots broke out with signs being raised comparing Jews to dogs and calling for the death of the Jews. When the region was under the Ottoman Empire, military and artillery were used to maintain order in Jerusalem, but now there was barely a warning issued to the Arab population. It was as if the British were playing a double game.

As the riots grew, so did crime, resulting in looting, robberies, rape, arson and murder. It took the British soldiers four days to bring the area back to peace. Surprisingly, growing support for the Zionist movement after the riots increased with the sheikhs and mukhtars who believed that Zionism would eventually usher in more industrial developments within the region.

During this time, an Interim Report on the Civil Administration of Palestine given to the League of Nations stated that "immigration and travel restrictions were almost universally applied only to Jews [but] no restriction was placed on Arab immigration." Furthermore, the report stated that "now in the whole of Palestine hardly 700,000 people, a population much less than that of the province of Galilee alone in the time of Christ...of these 235,000 live in the larger towns, 465,000 in the smaller towns and villages. Four-fifths of the whole population are Muslims. A small proportion of these are Bedouin Arabs; the remainder, although they speak Arabic and are termed Arabs, are largely of mixed race.

Some 77,000 of the population are Christians, in large majority belonging to the Orthodox Church, and speaking Arabic. The minority are members of the Latin or of the Uniate Greek Catholic Church, or, a small number are Protestants."

The Jewish people began arming themselves and setting up defense forces as they were not receiving assistance from the British government. It was even said that the British government later encouraged attacks on Jews. Col. Waters Taylor, financial advisor to the Military Administration in Palestine met with Haj Amin, the Gand Mufti of Jerusalem and told him, "[you] have a great opportunity at Easter to show the world...that Zionism was unpopular not only with the Palestine Administration but in Whitehall and if disturbances of sufficient violence occurred in Jerusalem at Easter, both General Bols (of Palestine) and General Allenby (of Egypt) would advocate the abandonment of the Jewish Home...freedom [can] only be attained through violence."

In 1924, more riots broke out in which 133 Jews and 116 Arabs died. Due to the economic woes at the time, Zionists began to request financial support from sympathetic supporters worldwide for their cause. Arab leaders, fearing Jewish economic dominance started more riots, even spreading rumors that the Jews were looking to take over Muslim holy sites.

On Friday, August 23, 1929, after the Jewish sabbath had begun at sunset, local Arabs in Hebron heinously slaughtered 67 Jews in the city. The rest of the Jews were driven out, thus ending thousands of years of Jewish presence in the city. Hebron, where the forefathers of the Jewish

Nation were buried—Abraham, Isaac, and Jacob—was now bereft of their descendants.

Other notable Jewish communities were also slaughtered and driven out, including the Jewish community of Gaza established during the reign of Maccabees, 2,200 years prior.

THE EVENING STAR, WASHINGTON, D. C., THURSDAY, AUGUST 29, 1929.

[BAR]LOW THANKS [ST]IMSON FOR AID

[Releas]e From Jail Is Regarded as Alleviating Dispute Over $9,000,000.

FREEDOM CLAIMED BY ARABIAN TRIBE

Flag of Turkey Is Raised by Moslems in Nablus, Palestine.

(Continued From First Page.)

At top is the Slobodka Rabbinical College at Hebron, 20 miles from Jerusalem, where 17 American students were reported killed in an Arab attack. Below is Jaffa Gate, the main gate in the old wall at Jerusalem, one of the scenes of rioting between Arabs and Jews.

The mounted figure at right is a Bedouin chieftain of the type who are leading their followers to attacks on the Jews in the more open country of Palestine. —P. & A. Photos.

[B]'S HOMER [BE]ATEN BY RUTH'S; YANKS WIN, 5 TO 4

LEO LOUGHRAN, 45, DIES AT RESIDENCE

Cigar Dealer Fatally Stricken at His Home Early This Morning.

LADY HEATH HURT IN AIRPLANE CRASH

Shuttle Is Forced Down at Cleveland As Oil Can Falls on Wing.

Box Score

FIRST GAME.
WASHINGTON

The Washington Newspaper, the Evening Star Describes the Brutal Murder of 70 Jews in Hebron Including 15 American Rabbinical Students. Aug 29, 1929 (13)

The British studied the catalyst for the riots and subsequently enacted the Shaw Commission which discovered that "the violence occurred due to racial animosity on the part of the Arabs, consequent upon the disappointment of their political and national aspirations and fear for their economic future."

Still, there was little effort on behalf of the British government to intervene in Arab riots, and consequently, the Arab leaders began to see riots as a very useful tool in building unrest and tension in the Jewish communities. Every time there was a riot, talks of halts on Jewish immigration was discussed. Jealous of the Jewish communities' external support and protection, hatred for Jews continued to grow at an alarming rate, even though the Jewish people still held to the resolution passed within the twelfth congress in which it was declared that "Zionism seeks to live in relations of harmony and mutual respect with the Arab people...[and to have a] sincere understanding with the Arab people."

Chapter 9: The Invention of Palestine - A Cocktail of Terror and Lies to Defeat the Jews

To this day there continues to be an argument for Palestine that is unwarranted and false. Every time a solution is even proposed, it is rejected because ultimately there is not a desire for peace, but for the destruction of the State of Israel.

In 1947, a two-state solution was proposed for a Jewish and Arab State, dividing the land in two. This was not the first proposal for a shared region.

For example, in 1937, the Peel Commission suggested a Jewish and Arab state. This was rejected by the Arabs, yet this did not stop other forces from trying to build an Arab population. British Secretary of Foreign Affairs, Anthony Eden, fought for the Jews to not have "any territory exclusively for their own use," even saying to his secretary, "if we must have preferences, let me murmur in your ear that I prefer Arabs to Jews."

MAP OF THE ROYAL COMMISSION'S PARTITION PLAN
(REPRODUCED FROM THEIR REPORT)
MAP No. 3

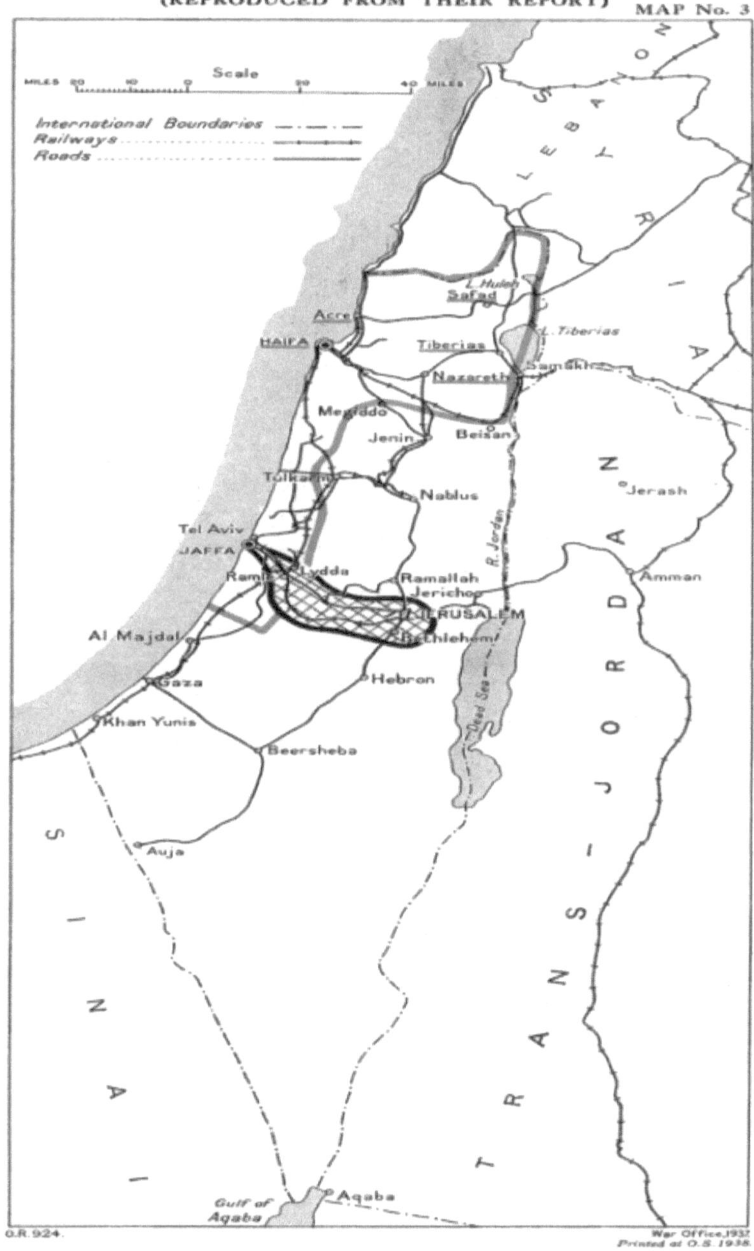

The 1937 Peel Commission Proposed a Jewish Micro-State along the Northern Coast and in the Galilee (In Red). The Jewish rejection was twofold: 1. Concern over Territorial viability. 2 Moral concerns regarding the proposed transfer of the Arab population. (14)

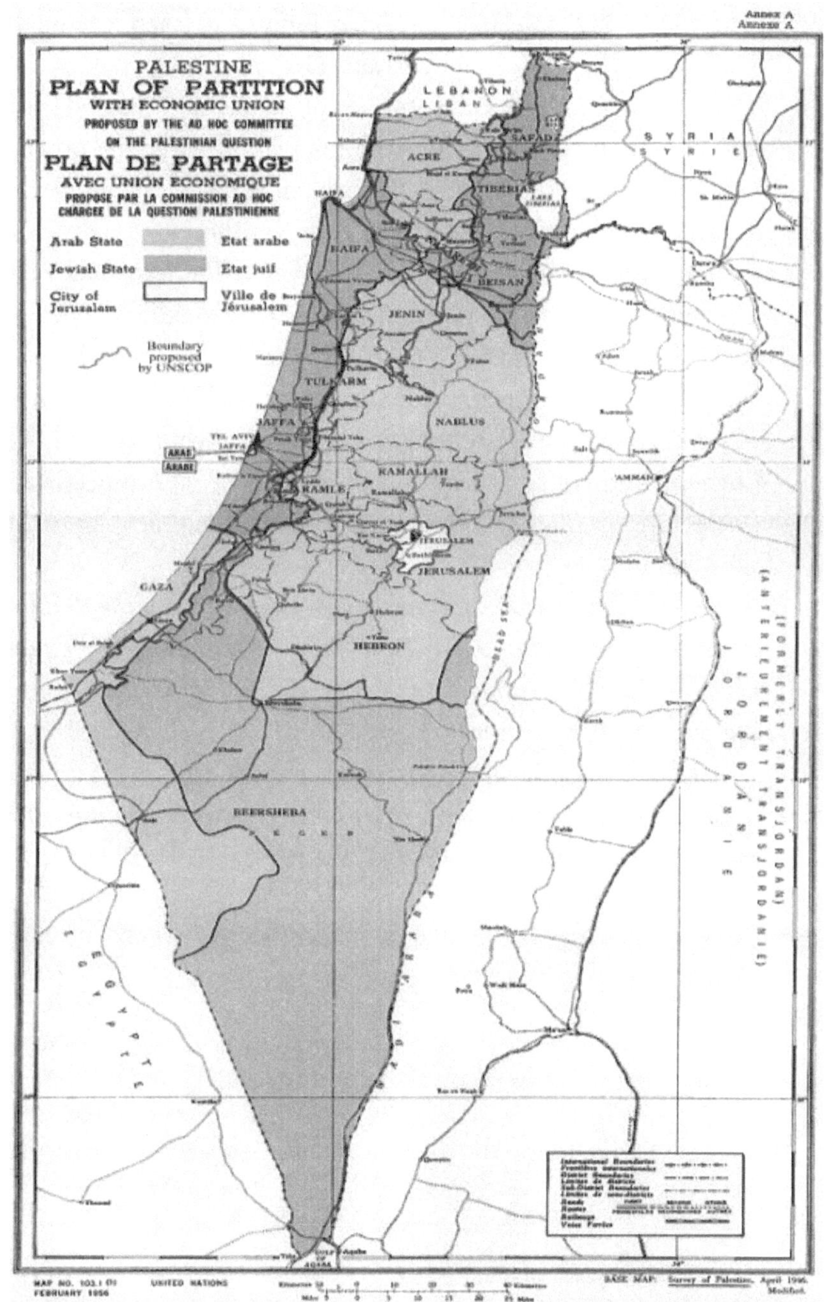
ANNEX A
ANNEXE A
PALESTINE
PLAN OF PARTITION
WITH ECONOMIC UNION
PROPOSED BY THE AD HOC COMMITTEE
ON THE PALESTINIAN QUESTION
PLAN DE PARTAGE
AVEC UNION ECONOMIQUE
PROPOSE PAR LA COMMISSION AD HOC
CHARGEE DE LA QUESTION PALESTINIENNE
Arab State
Jewish State
City of Jerusalem
Etat arabe
Etat juif
Ville de Jérusalem
Boundary proposed by UNSCOP
LEBANON
LIBAN
SYRIA
SYRIE
SAFAD
ACRE
TIBERIAS
LAKE TIBERIAS
HAIFA
BEISAN
JENIN
TULKARM
JAFFA
TEL AVIV
JAFFA
ARAB
ARABE
NABLUS
RAMALLAH
'AMMAN
RAMLE
JERUSALEM
JERUSALEM
GAZA
HEBRON
BEERSHEBA
NEGEB
EGYPT
EGYPTE
(FORMERLY TRANSJORDAN)
(ANTERIEUREMENT TRANSJORDANIE)
JORDAN
JORDANIE
GULF OF AQABA
International Boundaries
Frontières internationales
District Boundaries
Limites de districts
Sub-District Boundaries
Limites de sous-districts
Roads
Routes
Railways
Voies Ferrées
MAP NO. 103.1 (?)
FEBRUARY 1956
UNITED NATIONS
BASE MAP: Survey of Palestine, April 1946.
Modified.

The 1947 UN Partition Plan; Accepted by the Jews; Rejected by the Arabs. (15)

With the 1947, UN Partition Plan, it was said that 60% of the region would be given to the Arab population while the other 40% would be given to the Jews, and even then, 45% of the population of the proposed Jewish State was to be Arab. Furthermore, the area given to the Jews was mostly infertile and dry land. The Jewish Agency for Palestine accepted the proposition because they sought only peace, but the Arab higher Committee rejected it, just like the Peel Commission proposal and several other propositions to come. History continues to confirm how the Arab leadership is at odds with its own people. When the Mufti of Jerusalem, and ally of Hitler, Haj Amin al-Husseini went before the Royal Commission in 1937, the following exchange followed:

Sir L Hammond: His Eminence gave us a picture of the Arabs being evicted from their land and villages being wiped out. What I want to know is, did the Government of Palestine, the Administration, acquire the land and then hand it over to the Jews?

Mufti: In most cases the lands were acquired.

Sir L. Hammond: I mean forcibly acquired-compulsory acquisition as land would be acquired for public purposes/

Mufti: No, it wasn't.

Sir L. Hammond: Not taken by compulsory acquisition

Mufti: No.

Mufti Haj Amin al-Husseini with Adolf Hitler 28 November 1941
(16)

Mufti Haj Amin al-Husseini with Heinrich Himmler (Alber, Kurt) (17)

Another prime example of Arab leadership not acting in the best interest of their own people is revealed in an April 1948 police report from the British, proving that they were only interested in destroying the Jew and not in establishing a state. The report states:

An appeal has been made to the Arabs by the Jews to reopen their shops and businesses in order to relieve the difficulties of feeding the Arab population...at a meeting yesterday afternoon, Arab leaders reiterated their determination to evacuate the entire Arab population and they have been given the loan of ten 3-ton military trucks as from this morning to assist the evacuation.

The Jews asked for peace and the simple opportunity to reestablish their shops, not just for themselves, but to assist and feed the Arab population! Yet the Jews were met with violence via mortar fire and shootings. It's a shock that the Jewish population still wanted to help the Arab one.

In Ziff's 1938 book, he writes, "the amount of Jewish capital invested in this tiny land is estimated to total more than 120,000,000 pounds...in 1934 alone, they are estimated to have invested approximately 10,000,000 in Palestine. Today the productive output of the Jewish community is placed at 20,000,000 annually." He further expounds later on the fruition of this investment by stating, "The Jews point with pride to the fact that over 500,000 Arabs in the 12 years between 1932 and 1944 came into Palestine to take advantage of living conditions existing in no other Arab state. This is the only country in the Near and Middle East where an Arab middle class is in existence." What a statement.

During the 1948 Arab-Israeli war, 700,000, roughly 80% of the Arab's population fled from the land, resulting in what the Arabs would call "Nakba," which translates to "catastrophe." It has been compared to the holocaust by Palestinians but this is simply a lie. There was actually a mass attempted genocide upon the Jewish population, as seven Arab countries united against the one State of Israel. Many Arabs left at the behest of Arab leadership, which made it seem as if they were being exiled from their homes.

In the Statement to the Special Political Committee of the United Nations General Assembly, given by Ambassador Eban, it was stated that, "as early as the first months of 1948, the Arab League issued orders exhorting the people to seek a temporary refuge in neighboring countries, later to return to their abodes in the wake of 'the victorious Arab armies and obtain their share of abandoned Jewish property...that they would return within a few days [or] within a week or two, [their] leaders promising them that the Arab armies would crush the 'Zionist gangs' very quickly and that there would be no need for panic of fear of a long exile."

Palestinians did not appear to be worried about their land and the statement further sheds light on a reason why. It goes on to say:

"The Palestine refugees have the closest possible affinities of national sentiment, language, religion and social organization with the Arab host countries and the standard of living of the majority of the refugee population is little different from those of the inhabitants of the countries that have given them refuge or will do so in the future...unlike refugees in other parts of the world the Palestine refugees are no different in language and social organization from the other Arabs." Furthermore, "more than 50 per cent of the Arab refugees are under 15 years of age. This means that at the time of Israel's establishment, many of those, if born at all at that time, were under 5 years of age." Not to mention that "the [refugee] crisis arose not, as Arab spokesmen have said, because the United Nations adopted a resolution eleven years ago; it arose because Arab governments attacked that resolution by force.

If the United Nations proposal had been peacefully accepted, there would be no refugee problem today hanging as a cloud upon the tense horizons of the Middle East." In short, "the very origin of the Arab refugee problem indicates the difference. The tragedy of the Jewish refugee lay in his absence of choice. He was driven out by force or by decree and he fled from a real, not a mythical, terror. His only refuge was the remote 'homeland' which the Arab refugee left of his own will; the Arab was free to remain. There is a crucial distinction between fleeing to a land because of desperate need, and fleeing from the same land without need." (Syrkin, 1)

The Arabs left the area that was supposed to be the Arab state according to the partition plan (two-state solution). In the 1948 book, The Meaning of the Disaster, Syrian historian, Dr. Constantin Zureiq states, "Zionism is deeply implanted in Western life, while we are far from it...they live in the present and look to the future, while we are drugged-up dreaming of a magnificent past."

If the Arab population had a historical and passionate attachment to the land, they would not have been so quick to abandon it, even at the request of their leadership. This is in sharp contrast to the Jews who fought and clawed their way throughout history to maintain a foothold on the region, returning to it even when displaced in other countries. The call of the State of Israel has been rooted in the DNA of the Jewish people ever since the days of Abraham, while the Arabs see the area as merely dirt in which to place their feet. While many Arabs left due to the calls of their leaders, others left without such a command.

According to a local Palestinian Arab newspaper, *As Shaab*, the first to leave were the wealthy. It was written, "the first group of our fifth column consists of those who abandon their houses and business premises to go to live elsewhere. Many of these lived in great comfort and luxury. At the first sign of trouble they took to their heels in order to escape sharing the burden of the struggle, whether directly or indirectly." And in Tiberias, the Jews there were surprised by the sudden exodus of Arabs. The Jewish Community Council of Tiberias declared, "we did not dispossess them, they themselves chose this course. But the day will come when the Arabs will return to their homes and property in this town. In the meantime, let no citizen touch their property." (Syrkin)

The following drives home the point in proving that the Arab refugees did not have any real ties to the land,

"The Arabs did not want to submit to a truce...they preferred to abandon their homes, belongings and everything they possessed." - Jamal Husseini, acting chairman of the Palestine Arab Higher Committee (AHC), April 23, 1948

"For the flight and fall of the other villages, it is our leaders who are responsible, because of the dissemination of rumors exaggerating Jewish crimes and describing them as atrocities in order to inflame the Arabs...they (Arab leaders) instilled fear and terror into the hearts of the

Arabs of Palestine until they fled, leaving their homes and property to the enemy." - Yunes Ahmed Assad, refugee from Deir Yassin, April 9, 1953

"There is little doubt that the most potent of the factors (in the flight) were the announcements made over the air by the Arab Higher Executive urging all Arabs in Haifa to quit...and it was clearly intimated that those Arabs who remained in Haifa and accepted Jewish protection would be regarded as renegades." - Eyewitness account, London Economist, October 2, 1948

"...the fifth factor was the call by the Arab governments to the inhabitants of Palestine to evacuate it and leave for the bordering Arab countries...we brought destruction upon a million Arab refugees by calling on them and pleading with them to leave their land." - Prime Minister of Syria, Khaled al-Azem, 1973 Memoir

Even when discussing Nakba, the "Palestinians" are forced to remember it rather than being allowed to express how they truly feel. In May 2023, President Mahmoud Abbas of the Palestinian Authority declared that anyone who denies the Nakba would be jailed up to two years. All this does is further perpetuate a narrative and prevent the Arab population from digging into history's account for themselves. In the end, all the lies surrounding Nakba accomplishes is further antisemitism and unrest against the Jewish people. Antisemitism that gave rise to terrorist organizations such as the Palestinian Liberation Organization (PLO).

Although it stated that its aim was the liberation of Palestine, its actions proved to be far less innocent. First, it should be noted that the PLO was founded in 1964, which proves its fight was never about 1967 lines. Second, in 1968, it revised its charter seeking the destruction of the State of Israel. While providing little aid and support to the people it claimed to represent, it carried out numerous armed campaigns that resulted in massive casualties on both sides. This is in spite of the fact that even a founder of the PLO Ahmad Shuqeir, asserted that Palestine was nothing but Southern Syria when speaking to the UN Security

Council on May 31, 1956, stating that "history, law and cultural heritage supported his claim."

The first intifada (or "shaking off" in Arabic) started in 1987 when the PLO moved towards establishing a "State of Palestine," which was announced officially on November, 15th, 1988. Yasser Arafat was designated the president and moved towards a two-state solution. However, many of its members still looked for an excuse for violence, and in 1987, an Israeli vehicle hit two vans with Palestinian workers within them. Although this was not a targeted act of violence, this event was used as fuel for Palestinians. An Israeli man had been stabbed to death a few days earlier and the Palestinians perceived this as revenge on behalf of Israel, which was simply a lie.

Molotovs, rocks, grenades, explosives and rifles were fired at Israelis, resulting in almost 2,000 deaths. Rumors fueled the violence with no recourse, speaking of how young Palestinians were executed at hospitals and that water was being poisoned. All of these reports were found out to be false, but it did little to quell the violence at the time. It is a common tactic of Palestinian terrorist groups and authorities to incite their public to violence by libeling the Jews. The PLO did little to stop the violence. They would release pamphlets breaking down targets and declaring when violence should increase. As a result, however, nearly 1,000 Palestinians lost their lives, something that could have been easily prevented if the PLO and the growing terrorist group, Hamas, had not been driven by bloodlust.

To prevent the violence from escalating even further, both sides were encouraged to find a solution which resulted in the Oslo Accords.

In 1993, Israel signed the Oslo Accords, allowing the Palestinians to self-govern and maintain areas along the Gaza Strip and West Bank while the Palestinian Authority (formerly the PLO) would say that the State of Israel had the right to exist, however peace was hardly entertained on the part of the Palestinians. Hamas, in particular, rejected the Oslo Accords and carried out suicide attacks. The

Palestinian Authority (PA) also began building up their arms and military which was a direct violation of the Accords.

The years between 1993 and 1999 would become known as the Oslo War claiming the lives of over 300 Israelis and wounding over 2,000 via:

- Molotov cocktails: 2,499
- Shootings: 758
- Cases of arson: 115
- Explosive devices: 338
- Fragmentation grenades: 120
- Stabbings: 498

However, this was but a prelude to the upcoming second Intifada.

1996 Hamas Bombing of No. 18 Bus in Jerusalem Center killing
26 and wounding 48. (18)

(19)

On March 4, 1996, the Jewish holiday of Purim, an Arab from Ramallah detonated a bomb outside the busy Dizengoff mall downtown Tel Aviv killing 13 and wounding 130. It was the fourth bombing attack in 9 days claiming over 60 lives.

Tel Aviv 1900

It appeared as if a misunderstanding started a series of riots, but in fact, the second intifada was designed. Abd Elah al-Atira said in an interview with Palestine TV, "when he (Arafat) went to Camp David and saw that Jerusalem, or part of it, was not part of the deal (the Israeli-Palestinian peace talks), he [Yasser Arafat] came back and hinted to us to start the Second Intifada."

On September 28, 2000, Ariel Sharon, leader of the Likud party - a major Israeli political party, wanted to visit the Temple Mount - Judaism's holiest place. This also happened to be Islam's third holiest place, however, Ariel Sharon made special care to contact Palestinian authorities and inform them of his intentions. The authorities, including Palestinian security chief, Jabril Rajoub, let Sharon know that as long as he did not go into any of the mosques, all would be well. However, he should also note that the Palestinian police would not be able to protect him if a problem arose. Ariel Sharon made sure to bring Israeli soldiers with him for protection, went to the holy site during tourist hours, and gave no indication of entering any mosques.

Palestinians stoked fires by saying that he appeared with "thousands of soldiers" and said that the soldiers attacked Palestinians even though it was later discovered that no Palestinians were injured on that day. In fact, 28 Israeli policemen were injured from stone throwing. Further evidence of this was discussed in the Mitchell Report which came out on April 30, 2001, in which U.S Senator George Mitchell's investigation committee determined that "the Sharon visit did not cause the al-Aqsa intifada."

When more rioting broke out against Israel (a common and useful tactic on the part of the Palestinians historically), the Israeli police had no choice but to use lethal force, setting off events that would lead to the second intifada. Incredibly, despite their ongoing jihad against the Jewish State, Palestinian leaders continued to openly deny their own claims. During a shocking interview, while the second intifada was still raging, Azmi Bishara, founding member of the Israeli Arab Balad party, said, "there is no 'Palestinian Nation,' it's a colonial invention. When were there any Palestinians? I think there is an Arab Nation...Palestine was the south of Great Syria."

(https://www.youtube.com/watch?v=qy_PkZO1fcE&ab_channel=hebrewtuts)

Over the course of the second Intifada, Palestinians wounded over 8000 Israelis and killed over 1,400 more. However, their war on the Jews was costly, with Palestinian fatalities reaching into the thousands and the number of wounded into the tens of thousands. Even after numerous attempts on Israel's part to call for a cease-fire or peace negotiations, they were ignored, while some calls were met with even greater violence than before. There were hundreds of suicide bombings, shootings, stabbings, ambushes, stone-throwing and rock attacks. For example, a 10-month-old named Shalhevet Pass was murdered by sniper fire in Hebron while sitting in her stroller. She was shot in the head and her father was wounded in both legs. Or there is the story of Nava Applebaum, a young Israeli-American who was about to be married when she was murdered by a Palestinian suicide bomber. Her father, Dr. David Applebaum, also died in the attack along with seven others. He was known as the founder of the Terem medical centers across Jerusalem - establishments that treated Jews and Arabs equally. There was also the Passover Massacre, in which thirty people were killed and 140 were injured by a suicide bomber as they sat down for Seder. Hamas happily took responsibility for the bombing. There seems to be a theme of attacking Jews on their holidays.

In the aftermath, U.S President Bush said that "the Palestinian Authority [must] do everything in their power to stop the terrorist killing." Secretary of State Colin Powell said, "this is the time for Chairman Arafat to speak to his people, to tell them that they are destroying their own desire and vision for a Palestinian state living side by side in peace with Israel, behind secure and recognizable borders." The way Arab terrorism against Jews is criticized is concerning, as it's often portrayed more as a risk to the formation of a Palestinian State rather than acknowledged as a matter of historical and moral importance on its own.

The Remains of the Dining Hall after the Passover Massacre Seder Night at the Park Hotel in Netanya. 30 Were Killed and 140 Wounded (20)

It was not until the bombing of the World Trade Center on September 11, 2001, that Arafat, leader of the Palestinian Authority (PA), began to arrest terrorists and clamp down on the violence, fearing what the Bush Administration would do with the new heightened intolerance of middle eastern violence.

The intifada resulted in the economic decline of Palestinian Authority run areas and peace negotiations were halted. The influence of the PA is felt today, with young men in particular being persuaded by its past violence and hatred for Israel. Currently, they are jaded with the PA current desire to allow the State of Israel to exist and instead look to terrorist groups like Hamas or Hizballah for guidance.

Between terrorist groups, an aggressive Palestinian authority, and international religious and secular based antisemitism, Israel continues to fight for its survival.

Chapter 10 - The Greatest Lie Ever Told

In modern times, Antisemitism is still prevalent and spoken publicly, knowing that there will be little backlash to this heinous speech:

"They [Jews] tried to kill the principals of all religions with the same mentality in which they betrayed Jesus Christ and the same way they tried to betray and kill the Prophet Muhammad."

— Syrian President Bashar Assad, during the visit to Syria of Pope John Paul II

New York Post, May 6, 2001

"The Jews are the cancer spreading all over the world...the Jews are a virus like AIDS hitting humankind...Jews are responsible for all wars and conflicts...."

— Sermon by Sheik Ibrahim Mudeiris

Palestine Authority TV

May 13, 2005

"Let me ask you a question: Is it okay for us to talk about the coronavirus because it is 'hot news' and forget about the Jews, who are more dangerous than AIDS, coronavirus, cholera, and all the diseases of this world?...If you want to be saved from these deadly diseases, we should all remember Jihad."

—Jordanian Islamic Scholar Ahmad Al-Shahrouri

Yarmouk TV (Jordan), March 8, 2020

As long as support for the "State of Palestine" persists, there will continue to be a conflict surrounding to whom the land belongs, but the "State of Palestine" does not exist, nor has it ever.

When it comes to the State of Israel, it is clear that the Jewish people have claim to the land. There is a clear spiritual bond, a historical precedence, past political mandates, emotional and passionate longings to return and a long record of Jews only desiring their holy land to call home. Everything is connected.

Tel Aviv Today (21)

For example, the very traditions of the Jewish people are deeply rooted in their heritage, their DNA and their homeland, making it nearly impossible to separate each aspect from each other. Every facet of Jewish life has an origin tied to a deeply cherished and spiritual history in the land.

The Shekel, for example, is Israel's modern-day currency, but it stems from a long historical basis. The term shekel is recorded as early as the second millennium BCE in which Abraham bought a field and said in Genesis 23:23, 15-17, "I will give thee money for the field; take it of me, and I will bury my dead there. Ephron, the land-owner, replied: the land is worth four hundred shekels of silver...and Abraham weighted to Ephron...four hundred shekels of silver..." This currency wasn't made official until 1969 in which Israel voted in its government to change the Israel Lira to the shekel, taking even their currency back to their roots.

Meanwhile, the Palestinians are a non-homogenous group of people, of various faiths, languages and cultures that have no deep-seated connection to the land.

When Israel was said to have exiled over 1 million Palestinians from 1947 to 1949, a census taken by the British discovered that no more than 650,000 Palestinian Arabs could have been exiled, and this does not take into account the variety of reasons for their leaving. Wealthy Arabs did not want to be involved in war and many Arab leaders asked for the people to leave. Not to mention that if the situation was reversed, the Jewish people would have never left under similar conditions. Why did the Palestinians leave so readily?

Because their intention was never to create their own state, but to destroy the Jewish one.

This is not surprising. Throughout Palestinian "history" (which really only began with Yassir Arafat's rise to power in 1964), their leaders, whether it is the PLO, Hamas or others, have shown selfish attitudes towards their people, denying supplies, trade, advancement, and economic support to them. Attempts at cease fires and peace, whether local or internationally mediated, are met with apathy or violence. Events such as the second intifada are deceptively overblown to push a narrative. Lies, such as how many Palestinians were exiled in 48, are found to be inflated and unfounded. Over and over, Israel expresses a willingness to assist the Palestinian people, give them land, allow them to self-govern, and consider multiple solutions to usher in peace, but instead they are met with blood libels, incitement and war.

The big lie ...the lie that has been the cause of many lives lost, families displaced, and homes destroyed...stems from the false belief that Palestine existed and will rise again. The more nations that are educated to the history of the region and the Jewish people, the more that truth can prevail.

Advocates for Palestine continue to say that there needs to be a two-state solution despite the clear evidence, both historically and presently, that those in charge of the Palestinians do not want peace and would never entertain such a notion.

This could not be clearer than the results from the Palestinian Center for Political Studies and Surveys, taken at the end of May 2024, showing that even the Arab "Palestinian" public does not want peace:

- *73% of the respondents said that Hamas was right about the horrific attacks on Jews on October 7th*

- *96% of the Palestinians who did NOT watch the October 7th videos believe that Hamas committed any atrocities against Israeli citizens*

- *54% who DID see the videos do not believe that Hamas committed any atrocities against Israli citizens*

- *61% prefer that Hamas be in charge over the Gaza Strip after the war*

- *40% of West Bank Palestinians would vote for Hamas if elections were held today.*

- *Only 32% of respondents support a two-state solution*

- *52% say that an armed struggle is the way to end "occupation" and establish an independent Palestinian state.*

One of the major reasons for this? Religious ideology. Mosab Hassan Yousef explains in a video called the "Brutal Reality of the Middle East," the following:

"From the Islamic point of view...there is an Islamic trust that no Islamic authority can give [the land] away to non-Muslims. So when

the Jewish people returned to their homeland, the Muslims became outraged...that is the most fundamental reason and motive for the Arabs and Muslims to fight against Israel...they consider that territory as an Islamic land...the Jewish people have overwhelming evidence of artifacts and archaeology that supports their existence [for] centuries...millennia! But the Muslims don't. There is no currency, no book, no Bible, there is only a building that is 1300 years old [even though the Jewish temple beneath is older]."

The stunning success of the false Palestinian narrative proves that those who speak with absolute clarity about the justice of their cause, even if totally fabricated, win the PR war. While those who only speak pragmatically and apologetically are scorned and vilified. Until the State of Israel takes a clear stance and stops entertaining the notion that peace can be achieved through land giveaways...until it proudly and unapologetically calls out the Big Lie of Palestine—the conflict will never end.

References:

- Enemies and Neighbours: Arabs and Jews in Palestine and Israel 1917-2017 – Ian Black (2017)

- Israel at War: Primary Sources (jcpa.org)[1]

- https://guides.lib.uw.edu/c.php?g=341408&p=2298688

- https://sourcebooks.fordham.edu/mod/modsbook54.asp

- HUNTER, ROBERT E. "The Arab-Israeli Conflict." Building Security in the Persian Gulf, RAND Corporation, 2010, pp. 67–78. JSTOR, http://www.jstor.org/stable/10.7249/mg944.13. Accessed 12 Apr. 2024[2].

- Arosoaie, Aida. "Israel-Palestine." Counter Terrorist Trends and Analyses, vol. 7, no. 1, 2015, pp. 67–70. JSTOR, http://www.jstor.org/stable/26351320. Accessed 12 Apr. 2024.

- Troen, S. Ilan. "Israeli Views of the Land of Israel/Palestine." Israel Studies, vol. 18, no. 2, 2013, pp. 100–14. JSTOR, https://doi.org/10.2979/israelstudies.18.2.100. Accessed 12 Apr. 2024.

- Ram, Uri, and Jeffrey C. Goldfarb. "Introduction: The Culture of Conflict in Israel and Palestine." International

---

1. https://jcpa.org/publication/israel-at-war-primary-sources/?fbclid=IwAR13B-tet5kMHssxNsxiTmE3NliozVqMSUJZWnoj7EajbusWG7XJGf8ujxE

2. http://www.jstor.org/stable/10.7249/mg944.13.%20Accessed%2012%20Apr.%202024

Journal of Politics, Culture, and Society, vol. 22, no. 1, 2009, pp. 1–3. JSTOR, http://www.jstor.org/stable/40608201. Accessed 12 Apr. 2024.

• Hamas fighter says he is 'proud' of the October 7 attack on Israel and vows to keep fighting | News UK Video News | Sky News[3]

• Hamas's October 7 Attack: Visualizing the Data (csis.org)[4]

• Jean Doubdan's Le Voyage de la Terre-Sainte page 178 https://archive.org/details/bub_gb_K2xBAAAAcAAJ/page/166/mode/2up?view=theater

• Americans' Views of Both Israel, Palestinian Authority Down (gallup.com)[5]

• ICJ tells Israel to 'prevent genocide' in Gaza, rejects ordering immediate ceasefire | The Times of Israel[6]

• The Forthcoming ICJ Advisory Opinion on Israel/Palestine and the Doctrine of Illegal Occupation - Lieber Institute West Point[7]

• Commission of Inquiry finds that the Israeli occupation is unlawful under international law | OHCHR[8]

---

3. https://news.sky.com/video/hamas-fighter-says-he-is-proud-of-the-october-7-attack-on-israel-and-vows-to-keep-fighting-13004550

4. https://www.csis.org/analysis/hamass-october-7-attack-visualizing-data

5. https://news.gallup.com/poll/611375/americans-views-israel-palestinian-authority-down.aspx

6. https://www.timesofisrael.com/icj-tells-israel-to-prevent-genocide-in-gaza-rejects-ordering-immediate-ceasefire/

7. https://lieber.westpoint.edu/icj-advisory-opinion-israel-palestine-doctrine-illegal-occupation/

• What's the Israel-Palestine conflict about? A simple guide | Israel War on Gaza News | Al Jazeera[9]

• https://en.wikipedia.org/wiki/Timeline_of_Jewish_history

• 58-1.pdf (huc.edu)[10]

• The Encyclopedia Britannica 11th edition, volume 20. Pages 604-605

• They Must Go Meir Kahane.pdf (archive.org)[11]

• The Arab Refugees: A Zionist View – Commentary Magazine[12]

• Jewish Virtual Library[13]

• Hamas Minister of the Interior and of National Security Fathi Hammad Slams Egypt over Fuel Shortage in Gaza Strip, and Says: 'Half of the Palestinians Are Egyptians and the Other Half Are Saudis' | MEMRI[14]

---

8. https://www.ohchr.org/en/press-releases/2022/10/commission-inquiry-finds-israeli-occupation-unlawful-under-international-law

9. https://www.aljazeera.com/news/2023/10/9/whats-the-israel-palestine-conflict-about-a-simple-guide

10. https://huc.edu/wp-content/uploads/58-1.pdf

11. https://ia804508.us.archive.org/34/items/TheyMustGoMeirKahane/They%20Must%20Go%20Meir%20Kahane.pdf

12. https://www.commentary.org/articles/marie-syrkin-2/the-arab-refugees-a-zionist-view/

13. https://www.jewishvirtuallibrary.org/

14. https://www.memri.org/reports/hamas-minister-interior-and-national-security-fathi-hammad-slams-egypt-over-fuel-shortage

- They Must Go Meir Kahane.pdf (archive.org)[15]

- The Peel Commission Plan (1937) (embassies.gov.il)[16]

- The Arab Refugees: A Zionist View – Commentary Magazine[17]

- 11: Statement to the Special Political Committee of the United Nations General Assembly by Ambassador Eban | Ministry of Foreign Affairs ([18]www.gov.il[19])[20]

- SYRIA SAYS IN U.N. PALESTINE IS HERS; History Cited by El-Shukairy—Eban Derides Arguments and Sees Bid for Israel - The New York Times (nytimes.com)[21]

---

15. https://ia804508.us.archive.org/34/items/TheyMustGoMeirKahane/They%20Must%20Go%20Meir%20Kahane.pdf

16. https://embassies.gov.il/MFA/AboutIsrael/Maps/Pages/The-Peel-Commission-Plan-1937.aspx#_853ae90f0351324bd73ea615e6487517__4c761f170e016836ff84498202b99827__853ae90f0351324bd73ea615e6487517_text_43ec3e5dee6e706af7766fffea512721_In_0bcef9c45bd8a48eda1b26eb0c61c869_20July_0bcef9c45bd8a48eda1b26eb0c61c869_201937_0bcef9c45bd8a48eda1b26eb0c61c869_2C_0bcef9c45bd8a48eda1b26eb0c61c869_20the_0bcef9c45bd8a48eda1b26eb0c61c869_20Peel_c0cb5f0fcf239ab3d9c1fcd31fff1efc_remain_0bcef9c45bd8a48eda1b26eb0c61c869_20under_0bcef9c45bd8a48eda1b26eb0c61c869_20British_0bcef9c45bd8a48eda1b26eb0c61c869_20mandatory_0bcef9c45bd8a48eda1b26eb0c61c869_20authority

17. https://www.commentary.org/articles/marie-syrkin-2/the-arab-refugees-a-zionist-view/

18. https://www.gov.il/en/pages/11-statement-to-the-special-political-committee-of-unga-by-ambassador-eban-17-november-1958

19. http://www.gov.il

20. https://www.gov.il/en/pages/11-statement-to-the-special-political-committee-of-unga-by-ambassador-eban-17-november-1958

21. https://www.nytimes.com/1956/06/01/archives/syria-says-in-un-palestine-is-hers-history-cited-by-elshukairy-eban.html

- Fatah official: Arafat hinted for us to launch Second Intifada after Camp David | The Times of Israel[22]

- An Interim Report on the Civil Administration of Palestine to the League of Nations, June 1921 (eretzyisroel.org)[23]

- Who are the Palestinians? (eretzyisroel.org)[24]

- https://www.naomiragen.com/gaza-war-diary-13-june-2024/

- Guest Post: Were the Arabs Indigenous to Mandatory Palestine? — Indigenous Coalition For Israel[25]

- The Brutal Reality of the Middle East | Mosab Hassan Yousef | EP 443 (youtube.com)[26]

- Public Record Office, Kew Gardens, Foreign Office, Great Britain 371/20819

22. https://www.timesofisrael.com/fatah-official-arafat-hinted-for-us-to-launch-second-intifada-after-camp-david/

23. http://eretzyisroel.org/~jkatz/herbert.html

24. http://eretzyisroel.org/~jkatz/whopals.html

25. https://www.indigenouscoalition.org/articles-blog/1vp61ugv1lqoesdle18v62w0vrhc5i

26. https://www.youtube.com/watch?v=I5VPFw0vI6U&ab_channel=JordanBPeterson

Image Licenses:

1. (File:12 Tribes of Israel Map.svg - Wikimedia Commons)
2. (File:Kingdom of Israel 1020 map.svg - Wikimedia Commons)
3. (File:Kingdoms of Israel and Judah map 830.svg - Wikimedia Commons)

4.   (File:Hasmonean kingdom.jpg - Wikimedia Commons)

5.   (File:Carrying off the Menorah from the Temple in Jerusalem depicted on a frieze on the Arch of Titus in the Forum Romanum.JPG - Wikimedia Commons)

6.   (https://www.google.com/url?q=https://commons.m.wikimedia.org/wiki/File:Israel_under_Bar_Kokhba.jpg%23filelinks&sa=D&source=docs&ust=1720454312061421&usg=AOvVaw3FX8O8Sb45dUmiWAQZXyGk)

7.   (https://www.google.com/url?q=https://commons.m.wikimedia.org/wiki/File:Samaritans_marking_Passover_on_Mount_Gerizim,_West_Bank_-_20060418.jpg%23mw-jump-to-license&sa=D&source=docs&ust=1720454312057871&usg=AOvVaw1gaY0KuLuriSwy8rxPrfhg)

8.   (https://www.google.com/url?q=https://commons.m.wikimedia.org/wiki/File:Samaritans_marking_Passover_o

n_Mount_Gerizim,_West_Bank_-_20060418.jpg%23mw-

jump-to-

license&sa=D&source=docs&ust=1720454312052421&us

g=AOvVaw3OH3e_D0eKNOjOUejkvQEf)

9.   (https://www.google.com/url?q=https://commons.m

.wikimedia.org/wiki/File:BritishMandatePalestine1920.svg

%23mw-jump-to-

license&sa=D&source=docs&ust=1720454312051857&us

g=AOvVaw3k8S2oyZEx8OeZ02Z70ZoE)

10.   (File:Zionist-Pioneers-Early-Pre-Israel-Kibbutz.jpg

- Wikimedia Commons)

11.   (https://www.google.com/url?q=https://commons.m

.wikimedia.org/wiki/File:Declaration_of_State_of_Israel_1

948.jpg%23mw-jump-to-

license&sa=D&source=docs&ust=1720454312052758&us

g=AOvVaw1ovmjulJbZ60g-mD2tZ6QO)

12.   (File: Support for Palestine as part of Syria by

Arabs in Jerusalem March 1920.jpg - Wikimedia

Commons)

13.   (https://www.google.com/url?q=https://www.loc.go

v/resource/sn83045462/1929-08-29/ed-

1/?sp%3D2%26q%3DHebron%2BMassacre%2B%26st%3

Dpdf%26r%3D-0.211,-

0.07,1.422,1.422,0&sa=D&source=docs&ust=1720454312

063814&usg=AOvVaw0UjdJCKPjk2g33q7L4a2Zs)

14.   (https://www.google.com/url?q=https://commons.m

.wikimedia.org/wiki/File:PeelMap.png%23mw-jump-to-

license&sa=D&source=docs&ust=1720454312064097&us

g=AOvVaw3X0xyU96N9gB9gwS)

15.   (UN Palestine Partition Versions 1947 - United

Nations Partition Plan for Palestine - Wikipedia)

16.   (Heinrich Hoffmann • CC BY-SA 3.0 de)

17.   (https://www.google.com/url?q=https://commons.m

.wikimedia.org/wiki/File:Bundesarchiv_Bild_101III-Alber-

164-

18A,_Gro%25C3%259Fmufti_Amin_al_Husseini,_Heinric

h_Himmler.jpg%23mw-jump-to-

license&sa=D&source=docs&ust=1720454312055854&us

g=AOvVaw0FA4JP0FKoEytnJJGGtR0G)

18.   (https://www.google.com/url?q=https://commons.m

.wikimedia.org/wiki/File:HAMAS_suicide_bombing_in_Je

rusalem_on_25_February_(DoS_Publication_10321).png%

23mw-jump-to-

license&sa=D&source=docs&ust=1720454312057246&us

g=AOvVaw3pTqPO_v-i1NLsS4v8h6tf)

19.   https://www.google.com/url?q=https://commons.m.

wikimedia.org/wiki/File:Dizengoff_Center_suicide_bombi

ng,_1996_I_Dan_Hadani_Archive.jpg%23mw-jump-to-

license&sa=D&source=docs&ust=1720454312050706&us

g=AOvVaw3ufchM9HPavP4L0Gw0RYp7

20.   (https://www.google.com/url?q=https://commons.m

.wikimedia.org/wiki/File:Passover_massacre_II.jpg%23mw

-jump-to-

license&sa=D&source=docs&ust=1720454312051000&us

g=AOvVaw1NHX9BIFzZ8MtdSStjMex0)

21.   (File:Sarona CBD 01 - Wikimedia Commons)

www.ingramcontent.com/pod-product-compliance
Lightning Source LLC
Chambersburg PA
CBHW031748150726
47989CB00006B/2642